E Facile!
(It's Easy!)

Also by George Domino

PICASSO, MOZART, AND YOU: Unleashing Your Creative Self

PSYCHOLOGICAL TESTING: An Introduction
(2nd edition, Cambridge University Press)

E FACILE!
(It's Easy!)

A COOKBOOK FOR MEN

George Domino, Ph.D.

TUCSON ARIZONA

Copyright © 2012 by George Domino

All rights reserved. No part of this book may be reproduced or transmitted in any form or by any means, electronic or mechanical, including photocopying, recording, or by any information storage and retrieval system, without permission in writing from the publisher.

Published in the United States of America by:

Imago Press
3710 East Edison
Tucson AZ 85716

Library of Congress Control Number: 2012951549

Book and Cover Design by Leila Joiner

ISBN 978-1-935437-71-0
ISBN 1-935437-71-2

Printed in the United States of America on Acid-Free Paper

Table of Contents

How I Came to Write This Book 7
About These Recipes 8
Handy Hints 9

Appetizers 13
Salads 35
Soups 51
Chicken 65
Meat 95
Seafood 113
Pasta 127
Rice and Polenta 157
Vegetables 171
Beverages 199
Desserts 215
Bread and Breakfast 233

Herbs and Spices 247
Wine List 251
Index of Cooking Terms 255
Index of Recipes 259

This cookbook is dedicated to the best cook I know and love – my wife of 47 years, Valerie. She has had some excellent teachers – her Polish mother, Stella, and my Italian mother, Maria. In turn, she is a superb role model to our children – Brian, Marisa, and Marla, all of whom have turned out to be creative and versatile cooks when they can find time in their busy professional lives. To all of them, I owe a major debt for adding so much happiness to my life.

George Domino
Tucson, 2012

How I Came To Write This Book

I was born in northern Italy in a city called Torino, which many people, especially Torinesi, consider the cradle of good eating (the slow food movement started there). Unfortunately, I was born in 1938, at the beginning of the Second World War, and food was scarce, so the main concern of my family was not how good the next meal would be, but whether there would be a next meal. I can tell you that one of my childhood treats was a cup of hot water laced with a bit of sugar and, if we were lucky, a slice of lemon.

After the Second World War we migrated first to Venezuela, and then to California where food was relatively plentiful and of an incredible variety. My mother, whose self-image was measured by how clean she kept her home and how well she could cook for company, was an excellent cook. But like most women of her generation, cooking was a female activity in the home, and a male activity in places like restaurants and hotels, so I never got near the kitchen.

When I married in 1965, my wife turned out to be a wonderful cook, and even though she is not Italian (a minor imperfection in her otherwise sterling character...) she loves to cook Italian. As a professional nurse and mother of three children, her work schedule, both at work and at home, did not permit her to do much cooking except for special occasions, and even though I helped where I could with dishwashing, diaper changing, and other chores, her cooking opportunities were understandably limited.

I, on the other hand, had visions of coming home to a multinational restaurant where spaghetti Bolognese on Monday might be followed by Moo Goo Gai Pan, Hungarian potato dumplings, peaches in brandy, challah bread, boeuf bourguignon, etc., on different evenings. I decided that to make this fantasy come true (or a reasonable facsimile) I could either ask my wife to stop working as a nurse and stop taking care of the children, or I could learn to cook.

And so I learned to cook and found that most of it is not too difficult. You need to follow directions and not be intimidated. You will make a lot of mistakes, but most will still be edible. I collected a lot of cookbooks in the process, and eventually realized that most of them are written for women and/or by experts. I could not find an elementary yet interesting cookbook written for men whose professional lives do not center on food. And so, here it is: *E Facile!* – an Italian phrase meaning, "It is easy!" This book will help you approach cooking with all the excitement and wonder of a child who has just discovered that something that looks difficult, like riding a bicycle, is indeed easy.

About These Recipes

All of the recipes are for FOUR generous portions. Most likely you will have leftovers, which is much better than leaving the table hungry. If you are cooking for only one or two persons, the recipes can be easily halved.

These recipes were not chosen because they conform to the latest fad diet. Rather they are recipes that I like, are easy to prepare, and teach you something about various cooking techniques. I have tried to include recipes from a variety of cuisines, but I am sure my Mediterranean bias shows through. Although I am not vegetarian, many of the recipes (marked with a V) are, or can be.

BEFORE you cook, read the recipe through and try to visualize each step. If the recipe calls for a particular size pan that you do not have, try to improvise, but make sure you have the necessary implements. If you were building a bookcase you would need nails, but you could do a good job with screws or glue. The same analogy applies to cooking.

Once you are comfortable with a recipe, try to alter it, perhaps by using a different vegetable, a different cut of meat, or by adding or subtracting condiments and spices. Each recipe has a section labeled evaluation. That is for you to fill out. Was the recipe too salty? Too bland? Did you use a different type of olives? Did your guests like it? Was it served at a special occasion?

When you can, use FRESH ingredients. If you have your own garden or live in an area where there are produce stands, you will find some incredible differences between what is available there and what is sold in your local supermarket.

Finally, take a lesson from our Japanese friends. Food is meant to be enjoyed with ALL the senses. How the food is arranged and presented can be as important as how the food was prepared. BON APPETIT!

Handy Hints

APRON – wear one while cooking. It will save on laundry bills and give you a handy place to dry your hands.

CHICKEN BROTH – real "chefs" make the broth, called "stock," by using all sorts of ingredients. For those of us who do not work full time preparing food, there are two easier ways: 1) buy canned broth (chicken, beef, and vegetarian are usually available), or 2) make your own with cubes (sold in jars or packages, same three choices, you add hot water).

CHOPPED INGREDIENTS – you should realize that in reading recipes, "two tablespoons of basil, chopped" does NOT equal "two tablespoons of chopped basil." In the first instance you would have two tablespoons of basil which is then chopped, and would yield considerably less. In the second instance, you would chop enough basil to fill two tablespoons.

DEBONING CHICKEN – I prefer to buy the chicken (usually breast) already deboned if necessary. A bit more expensive but worth my time.

DESSERTS – Often because of lack of time or other constraints, it is not possible to prepare a dessert. There are however, a number of options: 1) a traditional Italian dessert is simply to serve fruit and cheese. A nice combination is pears with Stilton cheese (something like gorgonzola but more mellow). 2) A bowl of frozen yogurt with an assortment of cookies is always welcomed. 3) French and Italian pastries like Napoleons and/or cannolis from your neighborhood pastry shop. 4) Apple pie (with a bit of melted Cheddar cheese on top) is another possibility.

DRIED HERBS – when you add oregano, thyme, or other dried herbs to a recipe, rub the herb between your fingers as you place it with the other ingredients, to release the oil in the herb. As a general rule, dried herbs have a more intense flavor than fresh herbs, so use less. Where possible, add dried herbs at the beginning of the cooking, but add fresh herbs at the end of the cooking.

GARLIC CLOVES – to clean garlic cloves (the segments that make up a garlic head) simply take the clove in your hands as if it were a wrapped piece of candy and "unwrap" by twisting gently in opposite directions. The thin skin should fall off; if necessary, use a knife to pry the skin off. Or you can buy a handy gadget that looks like a rubber tube; you place the garlic clove inside the tube and roll the tube. Voila, the skin is off!

JUICE – when you are going to squeeze an orange or lemon to obtain the juice, first roll the orange or lemon on the counter back and forth a few times while you gently push down on it.

MEASURING – use measuring spoons and measuring cups rather than everyday spoons and cups.

MUSHROOMS – to clean mushrooms simply wipe with a damp paper towel. Cut off the end of the stem, which is dry. To slice the mushrooms evenly and rapidly, use an egg slicer.

PANTRY – If possible, always have cans of the following on hand: tuna; stewed tomatoes; corn; mushrooms; peas; anchovies; Greek olives; white beans; garbanzo (chickpea) beans. If you're in a hurry to prepare dinner and don't have the time to follow a particular recipe, you can simply "throw" something together from your pantry. For example, as that pot of water is heating up for the spaghetti, you can heat up some olive oil, some minced garlic, and a small can of mushroom pieces as a topping; 2) or in a bowl mix together a can of tuna, some chopped basil, a couple of tablespoons of lemon juice, and one or two chopped tomatoes – another wonderful "sauce" for the pasta.

PLANNING A MEAL – many of the recipes in this book are a meal in itself. Others may go well with a salad, or a side portion of vegetables. If you select two or three recipes to plan an entire meal, pay attention to how the various components fit together. A simple dessert, for example, might better accompany a rich main course. Dishes from different cuisines often do not go together – for example, spaghetti with Marinara sauce should not be followed by chili con carne.

PREPARING PASTA – 1) use a 10-quart pan filled about two-thirds with water. 2) When the water comes to a boil add one tablespoon of salt. 3) Add the dry pasta. Time according to the package directions, but use these as general guidelines. If the suggested time is 12 minutes, taste a strand at 11 minutes and continue tasting at one-minute intervals. Pasta should be "al dente" – not overly cooked and mushy. 4) After draining the pasta, don't rinse it, unless a recipe specifically instructs you to do so.

TO SEED – means just the opposite – i.e., remove the seeds. To seed an apple for example, means you would quarter the apple and with the knife, then remove the stem and seeds.

TO SERVE WINE – when you pour the wine, fill the glass only half full. As you finish pouring give a slight twist to the bottle – this should prevent any drops of wine from dripping on the tablecloth. To be doubly sure, you can buy a little gadget that looks like a ring that you slip on the neck of the bottle and it will absorb any drips; many of the newer bottles however, have a flared neck that does not accommodate such a ring. I simply use a folded paper napkin to unobtrusively wipe that extra drop from the neck of the bottle.

Appetizers

Bruschetta (V)

Special notes:

Sometimes the simplest things are the tastiest. This is the case with bruschetta, which is simply "country" (French or Italian) bread toasted (over an open fire, barbecue, coal), rubbed with garlic, and brushed with olive oil. You can make it a bit fancier and turn it into a nice appetizer by adding a topping, usually a mixture of chopped tomatoes, peppers, olives, etc.

Ingredients:

- 6 medium tomatoes, chopped
- 1/3 cup chopped fresh basil leaves
- 2 garlic cloves, minced (i.e., chopped finely)
- 1 tablespoon balsamic vinegar
- 1 loaf of crusty bread, sliced
- 2 garlic cloves, halved
- 1/3 cup olive oil
- salt to taste (optional)

Instructions:

1. In a bowl mix well the first four ingredients.
2. Toast the bread slices on a grill or under a broiler until they are golden brown (about 3 to 4 minutes on each side). You may not want to use the whole loaf of bread, depending on its size. Four slices of bread per person is more than sufficient.
3. Rub each toasted bread with half a garlic clove, and brush top of each with olive oil. Sprinkle a bit of salt on each slice.
4. Add some tomato topping to each slice.
5. Serve on a big platter or individual dishes.

Goes well with:

- Drinks: any red wine. I like Chianti or Bardolino.
- Other recipes: any pasta dish or salad as the main course

Notes/Evaluation:

Cantaloupe & Prosciutto

Equipment needed:

toothpicks

Special notes:

For a buffet, you might want to cut each melon wedge into smaller bite-size pieces, and wrap each piece with a small piece of prosciutto, secured with a toothpick. Prosciutto is a rather salty, well-cured "ham." If you cannot find prosciutto, you can substitute thinly sliced ham, or even thinly sliced salami, though the result won't be the same.

Ingredients:

- 1 cantaloupe (or honeydew melon)
- 8 to 12 very thin slices of prosciutto

Instructions:

1. Cut the cantaloupe in half.
2. With a spoon remove the seeds and center "debris."
3. Slice each half into four wedges and remove the rind from each wedge.
4. Wrap each wedge with a slice or two of prosciutto.
5. Use toothpicks to keep the prosciutto in place.
6. Serve.

Goes well with:

- Drinks: white wine like a Chardonnay or a Pinot Grigio, a Champagne cocktail, or even a dry (brut) champagne.
- Other recipes: you can serve this as part of a buffet, or a Sunday brunch, or even as an appetizer before the main course (for example, chicken).

Notes/Evaluation:

Caponata (V)

Special notes:

This is a traditional eggplant dish from Italy, with the French equivalent called ratatouille. The dish becomes more flavorful if it sits (in the refrigerator) for a day or so.

Ingredients:

- 1 cup olive oil
- 1 large can (28 oz.) tomatoes (do not drain)
- 2 onions, diced
- 2 green peppers diced
- 1-1/2 pounds of eggplant, peeled and cut into 1-inch cubes
- 1/2 cup red wine vinegar
- 2 tablespoons of capers
- 2 tablespoons of sugar
- 2 teaspoons salt
- 2 tablespoons tomato paste
- 1/2 cup chopped fresh parsley
- 1/2 cup pimento-stuffed green olives, rinsed and sliced thickly
- 1/2 teaspoon freshly ground pepper
- 2 tablespoons fresh basil, chopped
- 1/2 cup pine nuts

Instructions:

1. In a large heavy saucepan combine the first five ingredients (olive oil through eggplant) and cook for 20 to 30 minutes over medium heat.
2. Mix in the next nine ingredients (vinegar through basil). Cover the saucepan and let simmer for 15 minutes (if necessary, increase the heat slightly).
3. Let the mixture cool. Refrigerate if you are going to serve it the next day.
4. Caponata can be served cold, at room temperature, or slightly warm (but not hot). Before serving, sprinkle the pine nuts on top.

Goes well with:

- Drinks: any red wine; I like a Barolo, but a Merlot would do just as well.
- Other recipes: crusty French bread; follow with a pasta dish like ziti with broccoli.

Notes/Evaluation:

Cheese-stuffed Celery (V)

Special notes:

This is a very easy appetizer to make. Almost any type of creamy cheese or combination of a cream cheese plus a "flavored" creamy cheese (like those for bagels) will work. Among my favorites are Stilton, salmon-flavored cream cheese, and Gorgonzola; if you do use Gorgonzola buy it from a cheese shop and don't use the less flavorful "blue cheese." Don't use two "flavored" cream cheeses, since most likely they will lose their individual character when you mix them.

Ingredients:

- 12 celery stalks
- 1/2 cup plain cream cheese
- 1/2 cup of gorgonzola
- 1/3 cup of pine nuts or finely chopped walnuts

Instructions:

1. Trim the root part of the celery stalk; this will allow you to separate the individual celery ribs. Trim the leafy part. Wash the ribs under cool running water and dry.
2. In a small bowl mix the two cheeses well with a fork. This will be much easier if the cheeses are at room temperature.
3. Fill the ribs with the cheese mixture. Top the cheese with the pine nuts or walnuts. You can also mix the walnuts in with the cheese in step 2. If you like, you can cut the filled ribs into two or three sections.
4. Arrange on a dish and let your guests help themselves. For a fancy touch you can decorate the dish with a few cherry tomatoes and/or sprigs of parsley.

Goes well with:

- Drinks: gin and tonic; white wine like a Chardonnay or a Pinot Grigio.
- Other recipes: just about any other appetizers, in a buffet type spread, or as a nice, light introduction to a main course.

Notes/Evaluation:

APPETIZERS

Clams Casino (V)

Equipment needed:
pepper grinder

Special notes:
If you have some old dry bread (not moldy) you can make your own breadcrumbs simply by rubbing the bread against a cheesegrater. Otherwise buy a small container of bread crumbs.

Ingredients:
- 24 cherrystone clams
- 6 slices bacon
- 4 tablespoons of butter, softened
- 2 tablespoons minced parsley
- 2 tablespoons chopped scallion (use onion if necessary)
- 2 tablespoons fresh lemon juice (1 lemon)
- 1/4 teaspoon freshly ground pepper
- 4 tablespoons bread crumbs

Instructions:
1. Preheat the oven to 425 degrees.
2. In a pan over medium high heat cook the slices of bacon until crisp; crumble and set aside.
3. Scrub the clams under cold running water. Dry with a paper towel. Discard any clams whose shells are not closed tight. Place them in a skillet, cover, and place over low heat until the shells open. Discard any that do not open, and discard the top shells.
4. While you are waiting for the clams to open, in a small bowl use a fork to mix the butter, parsley, scallion, lemon juice, ground pepper, and bread crumbs.
5. Place the clams in a baking dish or similar container, spoon about 1 teaspoon of the butter mixture on top of each clam, and top each with some of the bacon crumbs.
6. Bake in a 425-degree oven for about 3 to 5 minutes, until the butter is bubbling.
7. Place clams on a large platter and serve.

Goes well with:
- Drinks: a dry white wine like Chardonnay.
- Other recipes: can be followed with any pasta dish.

Notes/Evaluation:

Clams Oreganate (V)

Equipment needed:
skillet
baking dish
pepper grinder

Special notes:
Although this is an appetizer, it can be a meal in itself.

Ingredients:
- 36 hard-shelled clams, such as "littlenecks"
- 1/4 cup parsley, finely chopped
- 2 garlic cloves, minced
- 1/4 cup Parmesan cheese, grated
- 1/4 teaspoon freshly ground black pepper
- 1/2 teaspoon dried oregano
- 1/4 cup dry white wine (like Chablis)
- 1/4 cup olive oil
- 1/4 cup bread crumbs

Instructions:
1. Scrub the clams under cold running water. Discard any clams whose shells are not closed tight. Dry the clams and place in a skillet. Cover the skillet and heat over low heat until the shells open.
2. Remove the clams from the skillet. Discard any that do not open and discard the top shells. Place the clams on the half shell in a baking dish.
3. In a bowl, make a mixture of the parsley, garlic, Parmesan cheese, black pepper, and oregano. Sprinkle the mixture over the clams. Sprinkle the clams with the white wine, olive oil, and bread crumbs.
4. Preheat the oven to 425 degrees, and bake the clams for 5 minutes.
5. Serve and enjoy.

Goes well with:
- Drinks: the same white wine used in the recipe.
- Other recipes: crusty bread, salad, pasta, chicken.

Notes/Evaluation:

Fagioli alla Toscana (Beans, Tuscan style) (V)

Equipment needed:

colander
pepper grinder

Special notes:

This recipe can be served cold as an antipasto, as a salad, or as a side dish. You can also use canned white beans instead of dried; if you do, skip the first three steps.

Ingredients:

- 1-1/2 cups dried white beans
- 3/4 cup olive oil
- 2 cups sliced onion
- 2 tablespoons freshly ground black pepper
- 1-1/2 teaspoons salt
- 2 tablespoons parsley, minced

Instructions:

1. In a colander wash the beans with cold water, and discard any pebbles, etc.
2. Place the beans in a 2-quart or larger pan, cover with water, and bring to a boil. Remove from heat and let soak for one hour.
3. Drain the water, cover with fresh water, and once again bring to a boil. Reduce the heat to low, cover the pan, and cook the beans for about 1-1/2 hours, until they are tender. Drain the water and set the beans aside.
4. In a skillet, over medium high heat, heat the oil. Sauté the onions until they are light brown.
5. Add the onions, pepper, and salt to the beans, and mix gently but well.
6. Chill, preferably overnight, stirring occasionally.
7. Sprinkle the parsley on the beans before serving.

Goes well with:

- Drinks: a light or hearty red wine, like a Bordeaux, a Barbera, or a Merlot.
- Other recipes: goes well with other appetizers as part of a buffet, or with a chicken dish as a main course.

Notes/Evaluation:

Flaming Kasseri Cheese (V)

Equipment needed:

a broiler (as in your oven)
a metal ladle or a small pan

Special notes:

You can use other kinds of cheeses besides Kasseri, but the cheese needs to have a strong flavor and consistency. Mozzarella, for example, can be used but just doesn't give the same results.

Ingredients:

- 8 oz. Kasseri cheese, cut into 1/4-inch slices (have cheese shop do this)
- Oil spray (or a bit of olive oil)
- 4 tablespoons Metaxa brandy (or other type of brandy)
- 1 lemon
- 1 loaf of French or Italian crusty bread (if you like, slice and toast it)

Instructions:

1. Turn on broiler in oven.
2. Place the slices of cheese on a metal surface that can go in the oven, such as a pan, a pie plate, cookie sheet, etc. To avoid having the cheese stick, place a little olive oil or oil spray on the metal surface.
3. Place the cheese about three to five inches under the broiler for about 7 to 10 minutes, till the cheese is soft and begins to bubble.
4. While the cheese is in the broiler, warm the brandy in a small pan or ladle; use a low heat.
5. When the cheese is ready, light the brandy, which should flame, and pour over the cheese (an appreciative audience is welcomed here).
6. Squeeze the lemon over each of the slices of cheese.
7. Serve with the bread; you can spread the cheese directly on the bread, or serve the two separately.

Goes well with:

- Drinks: Retsina, a white Greek wine that has a strong taste of pine pitch, but grows on you. Otherwise, a Chardonnay is appropriate.
- Other recipes : anything "Mideastern" that has pita bread, or a salad.

Notes/Evaluation:

Garlic Toast (V)

Equipment needed:
baking sheet
pastry brush

Special notes:
Use this to accompany pasta dishes.

Ingredients:
- 8 slices of bread (Italian or French)
- 4 teaspoons margarine
- 2 garlic cloves, minced
- 2 tablespoons grated Parmesan cheese
- 1 teaspoon chopped parsley

Instructions:
1. Preheat oven to 350 degrees. Place the bread slices on a baking sheet, and bake till the bread is crisp (about 8 to 10 minutes).
2. In a small pan melt the margarine, add the garlic and sauté for 1 minute.
3. Using the pastry brush, brush the garlic mixture on the bread. Sprinkle with grated cheese and parsley.
4. Bake until the cheese is lightly browned, about 2 to 3 minutes.

Goes well with:
- Drinks: red wine, like a Chianti.
- Other recipes: almost any pasta dish, like Spaghetti alla Bolognese.

Notes/Evaluation:

Guacamole (V)

Special notes:

Ripe avocados (a bit soft to the touch, but not mushy) are sometimes difficult to find. If the avocados are hard, place them in a paper bag, seal, and wait 1 or 2 days till they ripen (soft to the touch). Be careful when you mince the jalapeno peppers – you should wear rubber gloves (2 plastic bags held on by rubber bands work for me!) – or you can buy the canned variety.

Ingredients:

- 4 ripe avocados
- 2 tablespoons fresh lime juice
- 4 large tomatoes, chopped coarsely
- 1 or 2 jalapeno peppers, seeded and minced
- 1 or 2 garlic cloves, minced
- 4 tablespoons finely chopped red or white onion
- 1/4 teaspoon Tabasco sauce (optional)
- 2 tablespoons chopped fresh cilantro (Mexican parsley)
- 1/4 teaspoon dried oregano

Instructions:

1. Cut the avocados in half, remove the pit, and scoop out the flesh with a spoon. Place in large bowl.
2. Mix in the lime juice; this will prevent the avocado from turning brown.
3. Add all the other ingredients and mash well with a fork. Guacamole is typically a coarse dip rather than a smooth paste, so the ingredients should be slightly chunky.
4. Let it sit for a couple of hours for the flavors to blend (in refrigerator or at room temperature). Serve at room temperature with tortilla chips.

Goes well with:

- Drinks: cold beer.
- Other recipes: any other Mexican food; can be served as a side dish with enchiladas, tacos, burritos, etc., or as an appetizer.

Notes/Evaluation:

Hummus and Pita Bread (V)

Equipment needed:

electric blender or food processor
serving bowl
baking sheet
measuring cup

Special notes:

Tahini or sesame seed paste is available in specialty stores and mid-Eastern groceries. If you can't find any, simply toast 1/4 cup of sesame seeds in a frying pan. If you don't want to bother with the pita bread, you can buy packaged pita chips instead.

Ingredients:

- 1 can (15 oz.) garbanzo beans (chick peas)
- 4 tablespoons sesame seed paste (tahini)
- 3 tablespoons olive oil
- 3 tablespoons lemon juice (from 1 or 2 lemons)
- 2-3 cloves garlic
- salt & pepper

- 6 to 8 pocket (pita) bread
- 1 clove garlic
- 1/4 cup olive oil
- pepper

Instructions:

1. Drain the can of chick peas but SAVE the liquid. Place the first five ingredients in a blender; add 6 tablespoons of the chick pea liquid, and whirl until the mixture is creamy and smooth. (This step is best done a little at a time – i.e., don't pour the whole can of chick peas at once). This is somewhat like mixing cement or putty. If it is too runny, add chick peas. If it is too thick, add liquid. Towards the end, add a few dashes of salt and pepper.

2. Place in a serving bowl. This is a dip to be scooped up with pieces of pita bread.

3. Cut each pita bread in half across its diameter. Now you can split the two sides of the pocket apart, and cut each side into about 4 pieces each.

4. Crush the garlic and place in the olive oil. Now brush each piece of pita bread with the olive oil-garlic mixture, and place the pieces on a baking sheet in a single layer (you will probably need 2 or 3 baking sheets, or if you have only one repeat the following).

5. Sprinkle the bread with pepper. Bake in oven at 400 degrees for about 5 minutes. Don't let them burn. Remember also that it will take at least 10 minutes for your oven to reach that temperature.

Goes well with:

- Drinks: beer, red wine, Retsina (Greek wine).
- Other recipes: a good prelude to a soup, like Veronica's Mexican corn soup.

Notes/Evaluation:

Marinated Garbanzo Beans (V)

Equipment needed:

pepper grinder

Special notes:

A very flavorful salad that can be served as an appetizer, a vegetable side dish, or as a small salad to accompany the main course.

Ingredients:

- 1 can of garbanzo beans (drain)
- 1/3 cup red wine vinegar
- 4 tablespoons olive oil
- 1 teaspoon sugar
- 1 teaspoon (or less) salt
- 1/2 teaspoon freshly ground pepper
- 1/4 teaspoon dried oregano
- 3 tablespoons chopped onion
- 1 tablespoon fresh parsley, minced
- 1 garlic clove, minced

Instructions:

1. Combine all ingredients in a bowl.
2. Chill for several hours, so flavors can blend.

Goes well with:

- Drinks: beer, red wine or dry white wine.
- Other recipes: other appetizers; chicken or steak as the main course.

Notes/Evaluation:

Marinated Zucchinis (V)

Equipment needed:

electric or stove top frying pan
a glass (Pyrex) container that tolerates heat
measuring cup

Special notes:

This can serve as an appetizer, as part of the meal, or when placed on French bread, a delicious sandwich.

Ingredients:

- 4 lbs. zucchinis, preferably small and firm
- 1/2 cup salad oil (or olive oil)
- 1 tablespoon salt (or less)
- 1 medium onion chopped fine
- 1 bunch chopped fresh sage (about 20 leaves) or 1 tablespoon dried sage
- 1 cup wine vinegar

Instructions:

1. Clean zucchinis under cold water, dry with paper towel, and slice the long way into strips; strips should be about the thickness of a silver dollar,
2. Brown strips in an electric pan at 350 degrees using a bit of oil. Add oil as needed to the pan; the zucchinis should be frying in the oil rather than swimming in it! As each strip gets brown on one side, turn over to brown on the other side. When strips are brown on both sides remove and place in a glass Pyrex container. Sprinkle a bit of salt as each layer is completed. Repeat the procedure with all the strips.
3. When finished with all the strips, place the chopped onion and the sage in the electric pan. When the onion is cooked (it will be limp and slightly brown) add the vinegar and let boil for 1/2 minute. Pour the mixture over the zucchinis, and use a fork to allow the mixture to seep through the layers.
4. These zucchinis taste better when cold and when allowed to marinate (sit in the refrigerator) overnight.

Goes well with:

- Drinks: beer, red wine, dry white wine.
- Other recipes: I often like to make a weekend luncheon out of two or three appetizers, served with French bread and wine. The marinated zucchinis go well with the Tuscan bean dip and the marinated garbanzos.

Notes/Evaluation:

Marinated Zucchinis and Olives (V)

Equipment needed:

vegetable brush
glass pan
pepper grinder

Special notes:

Another variation of marinated zucchinis; this one uses raw zucchinis and calls for olives from your deli or specialty store (don't use canned).

Ingredients:

- 1 to 2 pounds zucchinis
- 1/2 cup olive oil
- 1/4 cup lemon juice
- 1 teaspoon dried oregano
- 5 garlic cloves, minced
- 1/2 teaspoon salt
- 16 to 20 oil-cured black olives (like Greek or Sicilian olives, grizzly or smooth)
- freshly ground black pepper

Instructions:

1. Clean the zucchinis using the vegetable brush, under cold running water. Dry with paper towel. Trim the ends, and cut into slices about 3 inches long (cut the zucchini in half the short way, and then slice the long way) and about the thickness of a coin (preferably a dime rather than a quarter, but watch the fingers!).

2. In a shallow glass pan combine the olive oil, lemon juice, oregano, garlic, and salt. Add the zucchini slices, mix well, cover with plastic wrap, and let marinate in the refrigerator for several hours, or overnight. Mix occasionally, so all the zucchinis get covered with marinade.

3. To serve, bring the zucchinis to room temperature (about 1 hour). Arrange the slices on a serving dish, garnish with the olives, sprinkle with freshly ground pepper, and drizzle with the marinade.

Goes well with:

- Drinks: beer, red wine, dry white wine.
- Other recipes: as part of a buffet, serve with other appetizers. Serve with breadsticks.

Notes/Evaluation:

Mozzarella in Carrozza (V)

Special notes:

In Italian a "carrozza" is a carriage or coach. How much more poetic than to call these fried cheese sandwiches!

Ingredients:

- 12 slices white bread
- 6 slices mozzarella cheese, about 1/4 inch thick
- 1 cup milk
- 2 eggs, beaten
- 1/2 cup white flour
- 1/4 cup olive oil
- 1 can anchovy fillets, minced
- 1 tablespoon lemon juice
- 1 garlic clove, minced
- 1 tablespoon chopped parsley

Instructions:

1. Trim the crusts off the bread. Place slices of mozzarella cheese to fit the bread. Make 6 sandwiches and cut each in half either in rectangular or triangle shape.
2. In a soup plate or similar container mix the milk and the beaten eggs. Empty the flour in a second plate.
3. Dip the sandwiches in the milk mixture and then the flour.
4. Heat the oil in a skillet over medium to medium high heat and brown the sandwiches on both sides.
5. Transfer the sandwiches to paper towels to drain the excess oil, and then place them on a warm platter.
6. To the oil in the skillet add the anchovies, lemon juice, garlic, and parsley. Stir with a fork and heat for about a minute.
7. Drizzle the anchovy sauce over the sandwiches.
8. Serve on a platter or individual dishes. If you like, decorate platter with parsley sprigs.

Goes well with:

- Drinks: red wine.
- Other recipes: almost any pasta dish.

Notes/Evaluation:

Peppers with Olives & Anchovies (V)

Equipment needed:

skillet

Special notes:

A simple but excellent appetizer. Red or yellow bell peppers are usually expensive, but taste much sweeter than the more usual green bell peppers.

Ingredients:

- 6 large red or yellow bell peppers
- 1/2 to 1 teaspoon garlic salt
- 1/2 cup olive oil
- 2 garlic cloves, minced
- 12 ounces pitted black olives (preferably from the deli, or from a can)
- 6 anchovy fillets, minced (just mush them with a fork)

Instructions:

1. After washing and drying the bell peppers, you need to remove their skins. There are several ways to do this, and all basically involve burning or steaming the skin off. One method is to broil the peppers as close as possible to a heat source. When the skins turn black, they can be rubbed off (by hand if you can stand the heat or with a towel). Or you can put them in a paper bag, close it, and let the skins steam off.
2. Once the peppers are skinless, cut them into thin slices, and discard any seeds as well as the white part on the inside of the pepper. Sprinkle the slices with the garlic salt.
3. Heat the olive oil in a skillet, over medium heat, and sauté the peppers for 2 to 3 minutes. Then add the garlic, the olives, and the anchovies. Saute for another 2 to 3 minutes and serve.

Goes well with:

- Drinks: red wine, beer.
- Other recipes: rice; chicken; pasta; use as a topping for bruschetta.

Notes/Evaluation:

Quesadillas (Cheese Tortilla Snacks) (V)

Equipment needed:

cheese shredder

Special notes:

Quesadillas are basically a melted cheese "sandwich," where instead of bread one uses tortillas. You can have endless variations by using different kinds of cheeses (feta, brie, or Monterey Jack are popular ones, as well as Mexican white cheese), by adding "spicy" ingredients such as chopped onion, garlic, Mexican salsa, pimentos, chopped olives, chili peppers, chorizo (Mexican sausage), etc. The procedure is like making a pizza, where you have a layer of dough (the bottom tortilla), then the ingredients, but then the ingredients are covered with another tortilla.

Ingredients:

- 4 eight-inch flour tortillas
- 4 ounces of brie cheese, thinly sliced
- 2 tablespoons thinly sliced green onions
- 1 tablespoon chopped cilantro (Mexican parsley)
- 1 small can diced chilies
- Tabasco sauce or some other hot sauce (optional)
- 1 cup shredded Monterey Jack cheese

Instructions:

1. Place 2 tortillas on a work surface. Add the brie as evenly as possible. Add sliced green onions, cilantro, chilies, and a few drops of Tabasco sauce. Add the shredded Monterey Jack cheese.
2. Cover each tortilla with another tortilla.
3. Heat the quesadillas until the cheese is melted. To heat the quesadillas you can use a microwave, any hot surface like a griddle, or a lightly oiled skillet (about 4 minutes on each side).
4. Cut each quesadilla into eight wedges and serve.

Goes well with:

- Drinks: cold beer (especially Mexican!).
- Other recipes: with a salad, this could be a light meal in itself; or a prelude to pork fajitas.

Notes/Evaluation:

Tabbouleh (V)

Equipment needed:
a sieve or colander

cheesecloth (like gauze and can be purchased in a package in most supermarkets)

Special notes:
This is actually a salad that is popular in Mideastern cuisine. As with most other recipes in this book, tabbouleh can be made in countless ways and can allow free reign to one's creativity. Here I present it as an appetizer. Bulgur is available in some supermarkets, as well as specialty stores like Greek delis.

Ingredients:
- 1 cup bulgur (crushed wheat)
- 4 medium tomatoes, chopped in small pieces
- 1 cup finely chopped parsley
- 4 tablespoons finely cut fresh mint
- (or 2 tablespoons crumbled dried mint)
- 1 cup finely chopped onion (if you have a food processor use it)
- 1/3 cup fresh lemon juice (about 3 to 4 lemons)
- 1/3 cup olive oil
- 1 teaspoon salt
- 1 head Romaine lettuce, separated into leaves (optional)

Instructions:
1. Place the bulgur in a large bowl and cover it with water. Let stand for 20 to 30 minutes. Meanwhile, you can prepare the other ingredients.
2. Line a sieve or colander with cheesecloth and drain the bulgur into it. Using the cheesecloth you should be able to squeeze all the water from the bulgur.
3. Place the bulgur in a medium or large bowl and add all the other ingredients. Mix well with a fork.
4. You can serve the salad directly from the bowl with pita bread slices, or line salad dishes with the leaves of Romaine lettuce and place a mound of the tabbouleh in the center of the dish.

Goes well with:
- Drinks: try mineral water (most wines don't go well with this).
- Other recipes: most meat dishes or eggplant dishes.
- Can be used as a salad – serve with pita bread.

Notes/Evaluation:

Tapenade (Caper and Olive Dip) (V)

Equipment needed:
food processor

Special notes:
This is a dip or paste based primarily on olives and capers – this is where the name comes from as capers are called tapeno in Southeastern France, the Provence region. Capers come in a small jar and can be found in most grocery stores, delis, Italian or Mideastern markets, etc. Look for small capers, about the size of a bb.

Ingredients:
- 2 cups black or Greek olives, pitted
- 3 tablespoons capers
- 4-6 anchovy fillets
- 2 tablespoons fresh lemon juice (from 1 lemon)
- 3 tablespoons olive oil
- 2 tablespoons brandy or cognac
- 3 garlic cloves
- 1 teaspoon thyme
- 1/2 teaspoon freshly ground pepper

Instructions:
1. Place all ingredients in a food processor and process until the paste is well mixed and smooth.
2. Place in a serving bowl and serve with pita bread, toast, crackers, or fresh crunchy vegetables like celery, carrots, and cauliflower.

Goes well with:
- Drinks: white or red wine.
- Other recipes: appetizers, or any main course.

Notes/Evaluation:

Tuscan Bean Dip (V)

Equipment needed:

food processor

Special notes:

This is very similar to the previous recipe, "Fagioli alla Toscana." For a difference I use canned beans, although fresh (dried) beans would work, perhaps even better. Which do you prefer? Some people don't like the sharp taste of raw garlic; if so, boil the garlic in hot water for about 5 minutes before you use it. Incidentally, if you used garbanzo beans in this recipe, you would be making hummus.

Ingredients:

- 2 cans (15 ounces) white kidney beans (cannelini) or similar (like great Northern beans)
- 2 to 3 garlic cloves
- 2 tablespoons olive oil
- 2 tablespoons lemon juice (from 1 lemon)
- 1/2 teaspoon salt
- 1/2 teaspoon white pepper
- 4 tablespoons chopped parsley
- 1 tablespoon pesto (optional)

Instructions:

1. Drain the kidney beans, but save the liquid. Rinse the beans with cold water and drain well.
2. Place all ingredients in a food processor and blend until smooth. If dip is too dry, add a bit of the bean liquid a few drops at a time. You might find that by adding one third of a can of beans at a time, the paste will blend better; sometimes the food processor cannot handle all the beans at once.
3. Place dip in serving bowl.
4. Serve with toasted bread (cut into small triangles), crackers, or crunchy vegetables cut into bite size pieces (you can use carrots, celery, fennel, cauliflower, etc.).

Goes well with:

- Drinks: red wine (I like Bardolino) or white wine.
- Other recipes: great with almost any main course, like the Piemonte pork roast.

Notes/Evaluation:

Salads

Caesar Salad (V)

Equipment needed:

salad spinner
wooden salad bowl
a whisk (or use a fork)

Special notes:

This salad is said to have originated in Tijuana, Mexico and is very popular (and expensive) in many restaurants. Traditionally, the salad is made at the table and you can do the same, although a bit of preparation is needed.

Ingredients:

- 2 eggs
- 2 heads Romaine lettuce, torn into small pieces
- 1 garlic clove, cut in half
- 2 teaspoons Dijon mustard
- 1 teaspoon Worcestershire sauce
- 2 tablespoons lemon juice (from 1 or 2 lemons)
- 2 garlic cloves, finely minced
- 6 to 8 anchovy fillets (1 can)
- 1/2 cup olive oil
- 1/4 cup grated Parmesan cheese
- 1 cup croutons

Instructions:

1. "Coddle" the eggs (this means gently cook them). So fill a small pan with water and bring to a boil. Immerse the two eggs using a slotted spoon, lower the heat, and let the eggs simmer for 2 minutes. Place them in a bowl of cold water to cool and stop the cooking. Crack open and pour the eggs into small bowl.
2. To clean the Romaine lettuce, wash the leaves under cold water, place in salad spinner and spin dry. Tear into bite size pieces.
3. Use a large wooden salad bowl. Take the garlic clove and rub the bowl with the halves.
4. Bring all the ingredients to the table and make the salad there.
5. In the small bowl whisk together the eggs, the mustard, the Worcestershire sauce, the lemon juice, the minced garlic, and the anchovies.
6. Add the olive oil in a stream whisking it into the dressing.
7. In the wooden salad bowl place the Romaine lettuce, add the Parmesan cheese, add the dressing, mix the salad well, and add the croutons as the last step.
8. Serve into individual bowls.

Goes well with:

- Drinks: mineral water with a wedge of lemon or lime.
- Other recipes: an elegant salad that can be followed by a meat dish like steak with cognac sauce. Bananas Foster would be an excellent dessert here.

French Garlic Salad Dressing (V)

Equipment needed:

an empty 16-oz. salad dressing type bottle (or similar container)
pepper grinder

Special notes:

This is a wonderful salad dressing that keeps well in the refrigerator. This recipe is enough for 8 to 12 salads. This is a very flavorful dressing, so use sparingly.

Ingredients:

- 4 to 6 large garlic cloves, peeled
- 3 (or less) teaspoons salt
- 1 teaspoon freshly ground pepper
- 8 tablespoons red wine vinegar
- 1 cup olive oil

Instructions:

1. Place the garlic cloves on a cutting board and sprinkle with salt. Mince the garlic with the salt to a fine mixture.
2. Take the empty salad dressing bottle, and place the garlic-salt mixture in it (use a small spoon, or a funnel). Add the pepper, the vinegar, and the oil. Cap the bottle and shake well.
3. Keep refrigerated, but let warm to room temperature before using it. Use sparingly on salads.

Goes well with:

- Drinks: whatever you have for the main course.
- Other recipes: French bread; almost any main dish.

Notes/Evaluation:

Greek Eggplant Salad (V)

Equipment needed:
food processor

Special notes:
This is a salad, but in texture is more like the caponata recipe.

Ingredients:
- 1 or 2 eggplants
- 1 small onion
- 2 large tomatoes
- 1 green or red bell pepper
- 3 large garlic cloves, finely diced
- 1/4 cup parsley, chopped
- 3 tablespoons red wine vinegar
- 1/4 cup olive oil
- 1/2 teaspoon freshly ground pepper
- 1/2 teaspoon salt
- 12 sliced green or black olives

Instructions:
1. Wash and dry the eggplant. With a knife, score the skin around the middle (the long way) so it won't explode in the oven. Place on a metal cookie sheet or other oven proof surface, and place in the oven a few inches under the broiler.
2. Broil the eggplant until the skin is blackened; turn frequently in the oven.
3. Remove from the oven. Let it cool, and then remove the skin.
4. In a food processor chop the onion, tomatoes, bell pepper, and when cool, the eggplant pulp. Chop coarsely.
5. Place the above ingredients in a salad bowl and mix well with garlic and parsley.
6. In a small bowl mix the vinegar, oil, pepper, and salt with a fork.
7. Pour the dressing over the vegetables. Add the olive slices on top, like spokes on a wheel.
8. Chill well, preferably overnight.

Goes well with:
- Drinks: Greek retzina wine.
- Other recipes: can be a meal in itself (with pita bread), or as a salad with a chicken recipe.

Notes/Evaluation:

Greek Salad (V)

Equipment needed:
blender (or an empty jar)
pepper grinder

Special notes:
If you like anchovies, you can add some on top of the salad as a decoration. If you like the taste of anchovies but not the way they look, add the anchovies to the blender when you make the dressing.

Ingredients:
- 6 medium tomatoes cut into wedges
- 1 cucumber, thinly sliced (discard the ends; peel if you wish)
- 1 red or yellow pepper, sliced widthwise
- 6 radishes, sliced
- 16 to 20 Greek olives
- 1/2 pound Feta cheese, crumbled
- 2 teaspoons dried oregano

For the dressing:
- 1/4 cup olive oil
- 4 tablespoons lemon juice (2 lemons)
- 1 garlic clove
- 1/2 teaspoon salt
- 1/2 teaspoon freshly ground pepper

Instructions:
1. In a large bowl combine the first seven ingredients.
2. Using a blender combine the last five ingredients to make the dressing. If you don't have a blender you can simply combine the ingredients in a jar and shake well – (smash the garlic clove before putting it in the jar).
3. Add the dressing to the salad, mix well, and serve.

Goes well with:
- Drinks: iced tea.
- Other recipes: crusty or pita bread; can be a meal in itself or followed by something like Chicken Moroccan style.

Notes/Evaluation:

SALADS   39

Insalata Caprese (V)

Equipment needed:

serrated knife (not necessary but useful)

Special notes:

This is a popular Italian salad, presumably named after the island of Capri. If you can get farm-grown tomatoes go ahead – most of the supermarket varieties have little taste. Chill the mozzarella before slicing – it is easier than if at room temperature. Use a serrated knife for both tomatoes and mozzarella to make slicing easier.

Ingredients:

- 6 large tomatoes cut into 1/2-inch thick (or less) slices
- 12 ounces mozzarella cheese (either plain or smoked), sliced into an equivalent number as there are tomato slices, about same thickness
- fresh basil leaves, one for each tomato slice (about 1-1/2 to 2 cups
- 2 tablespoons capers (optional)
- 1/2 cup olive oil
- 2 tablespoons red wine vinegar
- 1 garlic clove, minced
- 1/2 teaspoon salt

Instructions:

1. On a platter, arrange the slices of tomatoes (in a circular or spiral pattern), and top each with a slice of mozzarella and a basil leaf.
2. Sprinkle the capers over the slices.
3. In a small bowl mix the olive oil, vinegar, garlic, and salt.
4. Drizzle over the salad and let stand at room temperature for about 30 minutes.
5. Serve directly as a platter.

Goes well with:

- Drinks: sparkling water with a wedge of lemon; iced tea; a light red wine like Bardolino or Chianti.
- Other recipes: this can be a meal in itself, with some crusty bread. It can also be followed by a main course of pasta, chicken, or pork.

Special notes:

Notes/Evaluation:

Panzanella Salad (Bread and Tomato Salad) (V)

If you buy French or Italian bread at a bakery, you will find that the bread gets hard fairly fast, unlike American bread which doesn't seem to lose its texture for quite a while, thanks to the wonderful preservatives it contains! This recipe is a good way to use up French bread that is over a day old. You can add a variety of ingredients to this salad or keep it simple.

Ingredients:

- 1/2 to a full loaf of stale bread cut into cubes
- 4 large tomatoes cut into chunks
- 1 onion finely chopped
- 1 carrot thinly sliced
- 1 celery stalk thinly sliced
- 6 tablespoons olive oil
- 3 tablespoons red wine vinegar

Optional ingredients:

- 1 tablespoon capers
- 4 anchovy fillets
- 1 teaspoon minced garlic
- 1 cucumber, seeded and chopped
- 1/2 cup black olives (especially Kalamata)
- 4 fresh basil leaves, chopped

Instructions:

1. Place the bread cubes in a bowl. Cover with cold water and let sit for 30 or more minutes. Meanwhile prepare your other ingredients (e.g., wash and cut the tomatoes, etc.).
2. Squeeze as much water as you can from the bread cubes and place them in a large salad bowl.
3. Add all the other ingredients and toss well.
4. Let salad "cool" in refrigerator for about 2 hours before serving.

Goes well with:

- Drinks: red wine.
- Other recipes: can be a meal in itself, or can be followed by a pasta dish.

Notes/Evaluation:

Pepper and Onion Salad (V)

Equipment needed:

two 10- by 15-inch (or thereabouts) baking pans

Special notes:

Although this is a salad, it is more along the lines of a caponata, and can be served in small portions as an appetizer, or can be a meal in itself. Capers can be purchased in a small jar in many supermarkets, Italian or Greek delis, or specialty stores. If possible, buy the small variety, about the size of bbs.

Ingredients:

- 4 tablespoons olive oil
- 1 eggplant cut into 1-inch chunks
- 2 onions, peeled, cut into quarters
- 4 bell peppers (2 red and 2 yellow) cut in half, with stem and seeds removed
- 6 unpeeled garlic cloves
- 1 can (6 oz.) pitted black olives, drained

- 3 tablespoons lemon juice
- 2 tablespoons capers
- 2 tablespoons olive oil
- 1/2 teaspoon salt
- 1/2 teaspoon freshly ground pepper

Instructions:

Preheat the oven to 350 degrees.

1. In a 10- by 15-inch baking pan brush three tablespoons of the olive oil over the bottom and sides. Add the onion pieces and the eggplant chunks and mix so they are coated with olive oil.
2. Cover the baking pan with foil and bake for 45 minutes, until the eggplant is tender.
3. Meanwhile, lightly oil another baking pan, using about 1 tablespoon of olive oil, and place the pepper halves (cut side down) and the garlic in it. Place in the oven for 30 to 35 minutes.
4. When the peppers have softened (they usually collapse) remove the peppers and garlic pan from the oven, set aside the garlic, and cover the pan with foil.
5. When the peppers have cooled, pull the skin off and discard. Slice the peppers into 1/4-inch strips and add to the eggplant and onions. Gently mix the vegetables and let cook, uncovered, for another 20 minutes, until the eggplant is lightly browned.
6. Meanwhile, in a small bowl stir together the lemon juice, the capers, and the two tablespoons of olive oil. Peel the garlic, mash the pulp, and add it to the dressing.

7. When the vegetables are cooked, add the dressing, the olives, the salt, and the pepper. Mix well.
8. Let cool. This salad can be served either lukewarm or chilled. Best prepared the day ahead and chilled for tastes to blend.

Goes well with:
- Drinks: red wine.
- Other recipes: goes well with other appetizers, or as a salad with a chicken dish.

Notes/Evaluation:

Salad Nicoise (V)

Equipment needed:

egg slicer
large platter
colander

Special notes:

This is another classical recipe, from the Southern coast of France (the city of Nice). There are endless variations of this salad, but the salad typically includes tomatoes, olives, potatoes, anchovies, and canned tuna. Traditionally, the ingredients are not mixed but are arranged artistically on a large platter.

Ingredients:

- 2 tablespoons salt
- 1 pound green beans, washed and ends trimmed
- 6 small red-skinned potatoes
- 2 green peppers
- 1 small red onion
- 4 hard boiled eggs (see step #5)
- 2 cans of tuna (6 ounces each)
- 1 cup pitted green olives
- 2 tablespoons chopped fresh basil

For the dressing:

- 2 teaspoons Dijon mustard
- 2 tablespoons red wine vinegar
- 2 garlic cloves, finely minced
- 4 anchovy fillets
- 1/2 teaspoon dried thyme
- 1 teaspoon salt
- 1/2 teaspoon freshly ground pepper
- 6 tablespoons olive oil

Instructions:

1. Bring a large pot of water to a boil. Add one tablespoon of salt to the water. Add the green beans and cook 3 to 5 minutes – they should be crisp, not soft. Drain into a colander, run under cool water and set aside.

2. Bring a large pot of water to a boil. Add one tablespoon of salt and the six potatoes. Cook for approximately 20 minutes until tender (stick one with a fork to determine if tender). Drain, let cool, and slice into bite size pieces. (If you are brave, and have 2 pots, you can carry out steps #1 and steps #2 at the same time!).

3. Slice the green peppers either lengthwise or widthwise. Discard the stem, seeds, and any white membrane. Set aside.

4. Slice the onion as thinly as possible. Throw out outer layer.

5. To hard boil the eggs: fill a saucepan 1/2 to 2/3 with water and bring to a boil. Using a slotted spoon submerge the eggs into the water, lower the heat, and simmer for 13 to 15 minutes. Remove the eggs and place them in cold water. You might even want to add some ice cubes to the water to have it really cold. Remove the shells from the egg by gently and repeatedly cracking the shell on a flat surface. The shell should be easy to remove. If necessary, "wash" the egg under cold water to remove any bits of shell. Use an egg slicer to cut the eggs into uniform slices.

6. On a large platter arrange the beans, potatoes, peppers, onion, eggs, tuna, and green olives. Sprinkle the fresh basil over the potatoes.

7. Make the dressing. In a small bowl mix all the ingredients with a fork. Add the oil last in a steady stream, whisking it with the fork.

8. Drizzle the dressing over the salad. Let each guest select what they want.

Goes well with:

- Drinks: red wine.
- Other recipes: this is a robust salad that can be a meal in itself. For a "soup and salad" type dinner, follow with a light soup like Stracciatella alla Romana.

Notes/Evaluation:

Salad with Honey Mustard Vinaigrette (V)

Equipment needed:
blender (or large jar)

Special notes:
If you don't have a blender you can achieve the same results with a jar that has a tight-fitting kid. Simply add the ingredients in the jar and shake well. As always, add the olive oil last and in small quantities, so the oil can blend in. Incidentally, a vinaigrette is a simple but classic French dressing that usually consists of 3 or 4 parts olive oil to one part vinegar, with salt and pepper, and perhaps other ingredients like garlic or mustard. If you've ever ordered a salad in a restaurant, most likely you were served iceberg lettuce; there is nothing wrong with it; it is fairly standard, but also quite boring. For this recipe, try using some different greens.

Ingredients:
- 8 to 10 cups of mixed greens (you can buy these already cut and mixed, or you can buy the individual greens like romaine, endive, arugula, escarole, and even Bok Choi (Chinese cabbage)

For the vinaigrette:
- 2 tablespoons white wine vinegar
- 2 tablespoons fresh lemon juice (from 1 lemon)
- 1-1/2 teaspoons Dijon-style mustard
- 1 tablespoon honey
- 1/2 teaspoon salt
- 1/2 teaspoon ground black pepper
- 6 to 8 tablespoons olive oil

Instructions:
1. Prepare the greens if you need to (i.e., wash and dry; tear into pieces).
2. In a blender (or jar) mix the ingredients for the vinaigrette, except for the olive oil. Add the olive oil slowly to the dressing, a little at a time while the blender is running.
3. Add the dressing to the salad, mix well, and serve.

Goes well with:
- Drinks: iced tea.
- Other recipe: this is a "standard" salad that can precede just about any main course. On summer days (or if you're trying to lose weight) this can be a meal in itself. Feel free to jazz it up with sliced cucumber, and/or baby carrots, radishes, chopped celery, canned garbanzo beans, and whatever else you fancy. Crusty bread goes great!

Notes/Evaluation:

Tomato and Basil Salad (V)

Equipment needed:

pepper grinder

Special notes:

An ideal summer salad, especially with tomatoes and basil fresh from the garden.

Ingredients:

- 4 to 6 large ripe tomatoes
- 2 tablespoons red wine vinegar
- 4 tablespoons olive oil
- 1/2 teaspoon salt
- 1/2 teaspoon freshly ground black pepper
- 4 to 6 fresh basil leaves, minced (or 1 tablespoon dried basil flakes)

Instructions:

1. If you wish to peel the tomatoes, dip them in a pan of boiling water for about 30 to 45 seconds. Rinse them with cool water and peel the skin. (Some people do not like the skin of tomatoes; I have no problem skipping this step).
2. Slice the tomatoes and arrange the slices on a serving platter (overlapping them in a circular pattern is one possibility).
3. In a jar or bottle combine the vinegar, oil, salt, and pepper. Shake vigorously (make sure the top is on tightly), and sprinkle over the tomatoes. Sprinkle with minced basil leaves.
4. Let marinate about 60 minutes at room temperature and serve.

Goes well with:

- Drinks: red or white (dry) wine.
- Other recipes: French bread, almost any main dish.

Notes/Evaluation:

SALADS

Tomato Salad (V)

Equipment needed:

pepper grinder

Special notes:

You can change this salad in many ways, depending on the ingredients you have available; you could, for example, add sliced carrots, celery, Monterey Jack cheese, pepperoncinis (Italian pickled peppers), etc. This is a good summer dish.

Ingredients:

- 8 to 12 tomatoes (more if small, less if large), sliced
- 1 or 2 cucumbers, peeled and sliced thinly
- 1/2 teaspoon marjoram (a spice)
- 1/2 teaspoon oregano (another spice)
- 1/2 teaspoon salt
- 1/2 teaspoon freshly ground pepper
- fresh basil leaves (1 per tomato slice) (or 1/2 teaspoon dry)
- 1 tablespoon capers (found in small jar in gourmet section of grocery store)
- olives – any kind you wish, green, black, Kalamata, etc., whole or sliced
- virgin olive oil
- red wine vinegar
- lemon juice

Instructions:

1. Take a large serving platter and on it arrange the tomato slices, and on top of that the cucumber slices, and the fresh basil leaves (if you are using them).
2. Mix well the marjoram, oregano, salt, and pepper and sprinkle over the tomato/cucumber slices.
3. Add the capers and the olives, and sprinkle the olive oil, the vinegar and the lemon juice (more oil than vinegar or lemon juice – on the proportion of 8 tablespoons olive oil to 1 of vinegar and 1 of lemon juice).
4. Cover with plastic wrap and chill for 1 or 2 hours.

Goes well with:

- Drinks: iced tea, beer, wine, sparkling water (like San Pellegrino).
- Other recipes: this can be a meal in itself or, served as smaller portions, a prelude to chicken, pasta, etc.

Notes/Evaluation:

Waldorf Salad (V)

Special notes:

This salad was originally created at the Waldorf-Astoria Hotel in New York City in the late 1800's. Basically, it is made up of apples, celery, and mayonnaise, though most recipes also include walnuts.

Ingredients:

- 2 pounds Delicious red apples (Delicious is the varietal name)
- 1 tablespoon fresh lemon juice (1 lemon)
- 1-1/2 cups sliced celery
- 1 cup walnuts, chopped coarsely
- 1/2 to 3/4 cup mayonnaise
- 4 to 8 lettuce leaves, washed and dried (optional)

Instructions:

1. Wash and pat dry the apples. If you want to you can peel them. Cut in quarters and remove the stem, seeds, and center part (this is what recipes mean when they say "core" the apples). Cut the quarters into coarse bite size pieces.
2. In a bowl mix the apples well with the lemon juice to prevent discoloration.
3. Add the sliced celery, walnuts, and mayonnaise, and mix well.
4. If you wish, line salad dishes with the lettuce leaves and place spoonfuls of salad on the leaves. Serve.

Goes well with:

- Drinks: mineral water with a slice of lemon.
- Other recipes: this is a "heavy" salad and small servings are best. Good followed by a chicken recipe.

Notes/Evaluation:

Soups

Albondigas Soup (Mexican Meatball Soup)

Special notes:

A Spanish instructor at the University once told me that the word "albondigas" was translated by one of his beginning students as "give gas to the good God" … For the broth, you can buy canned or make your own out of bouillon cubes; just follow the directions on the jar of bouillon cubes.

Ingredients:

- 2 tablespoons cooking (salad) oil
- 1 medium onion, chopped
- 2 cloves of garlic, minced
- 1 small (14.5 oz.) can of peeled or crushed tomatoes
- 8 to 10 cups beef broth
- 2 carrots sliced the thickness of a dime
- 2 potatoes, peeled and cut into cubes about 1/2-inch in size
- 1 bay leaf
- 2 limes cut into wedges

Ingredients for meatballs:

- 1 egg
- 1/2 teaspoon dried oregano
- 1/4 cup cilantro (or parsley)
- 1/2 teaspoon salt
- 1/4 teaspoon freshly ground pepper
- 1/4 cup rice, uncooked
- 3/4 pound ground lean beef
- 3/4 pound bulk pork sausage

Instructions:

1. Heat the oil in a 6-quart pan over medium heat; it will take 3 to 5 minutes. When the oil is hot, add the onion and garlic. Stir and sauté for about 10 to 15 minutes, until the onion is tender and golden.

2. Add the tomatoes; if chunky, break them up. Add the broth and bring to a boil. Add the carrots, potatoes, and bay leaf. Simmer the soup for about 5 to 7 minutes.

3. While the soup is heating (step #2) make the meatballs. In a bowl beat the egg well and combine with the oregano, cilantro, salt and pepper. Now add the rice, the ground beef, and the pork sausage. Mix well (the best way to do this is with your clean fingers). Shape the mixture into meatballs, about 1 to 1 & 1/2 inch in diameter (about the size of a golf ball).

4. Add the meatballs, a few at a time, to the simmering soup. Increase the heat till the soup begins to boil. Reduce the heat and simmer for 30 to 40 minutes till the vegetables and the meatballs are done.

5. Remove the bay leaf before serving. Serve. Have slices of lime available if anyone wants to squeeze some lime juice on top of the soup.

Goes well with:
- Drinks: cold beer.
- Other recipes: any other Mexican food.

Notes/Evaluation:

Bean Soup alla Bolognese (V)

Equipment needed:
colander or sieve
electric blender

Special notes:
Bologna is a city in northeastern Italy famous for its university as well as for its food. To crush the garlic you can use a garlic crusher or the flat blade of a large knife.

Ingredients:
- 2 cups dried white beans
- 2-1/2 quarts water
- 1 can (14-1/2 oz.) chopped tomatoes (you can also use stewed tomatoes or plum tomatoes)
- 2 garlic cloves, crushed
- 2 bay leaves
- 2 cubes of vegetarian (or beef) bouillon
- 2 tablespoons virgin olive oil
- 1/2 cup finely chopped onion
- garlic cloves, finely minced
- 1/2 teaspoon salt (optional)
- 1/2 teaspoon freshly ground pepper (optional)

Instructions:
1. Wash the beans under cool running water in a colander or sieve.
2. Place the beans in a 6-quart pot and fill 1/2 to 1/3 with water. Bring to a boil, remove from heat, and let sit for one hour.
3. Drain the beans, put back in pot, add 2-1/2 quarts of water, the chopped tomatoes, the crushed garlic, the bay leaves, and the two bouillon cubes. Bring to a boil and then simmer over low heat for 2 to 2-1/2 hours till the beans are tender.
4. Discard the bay leaves. Using an electric blender or a sieve, puree about half of the bean mixture. Return the puree to the pot.
5. In a skillet heat the oil and sauté the onions for about ten minutes over medium heat. Add the minced garlic and sauté for about two more minutes.
6. Add the onion and garlic to the soup, mix well, and simmer for about 20 more minutes.
7. Add the salt and pepper if needed. Serve.

Goes well with:
- Drinks: red wine (Chianti would be good).
- Other recipes: serve with crusty bread. A good soup to pair with a salad, or to serve with a chicken dish like pollo all'aglio.

Notes/Evaluation:

French Onion Soup (V)

Equipment needed:

a broiler
a heavy 6-quart pot

Special notes:

You can use vegetarian broth rather than beef broth if you wish. Gruyere cheese can be purchased at a cheese shop – it has a wonderful nutty taste; buy some extra and just eat it with French bread! This recipe requires thinly slicing some two pounds of onions. Don't believe what cookbooks tell you about slicing the onions under water to avoid crying. The best advice I can give you is to stand back as far as it is safe to do, but you will probably end up crying – it builds character…

Ingredients:

- 1-1/2 to 2 pounds onions, thinly sliced
- 1 tablespoon virgin olive oil
- 3 tablespoons butter
- 8 cups beef broth (or vegetarian broth)
- 8 slices French bread
- 4 garlic cloves, each cut in half
- 3 tablespoons virgin olive oil
- 1 cup (about 4 ounces) grated Gruyere cheese
- 1/2 cup of Port or Sherry wine (optional)

Instructions:

1. In a heavy 6-quart pot, heat the oil and butter over medium heat. Add the onions and sauté for 15 to 20 minutes, stirring occasionally, until the onions are lightly browned.
2. Add the broth, bring to a boil, and simmer for about 10 minutes.
3. While the soup simmers, toast the bread. If the slices are thin, you can use a regular toaster. If they are thick and your toaster does not handle them, you might need a broiler.
4. Rub each slice of toasted bread with a cut garlic clove and lightly brush each slice with olive oil. Top each slice of bread with a handful of cheese and place under broiler until the cheese melts.
5. In each soup bowl place a slice of the toasted bread with the melted cheese and ladle the soup. If you wish, add a shot of the Port or Sherry to each bowl. (Or try a few drops of Worcestershire sauce for an added zing.)

Goes well with:

- Drinks: sherry or port wine.
- Other recipes: great with Chicken with Mushrooms.

Notes/Evaluation:

Greek Avgolemono Soup (V)

Equipment needed:

a whisk or a rotary beater, or an electric mixer

Special notes:

You can buy canned chicken broth (preferably low salt), or you can make your own using chicken cubes (available in most supermarkets). For a vegetarian version use vegetable rather than chicken broth (also available already made or in concentrated cubes).

Ingredients:

- 8-10 cups chicken (or vegetable) broth
- 1/2 cup rice
- 4 eggs
- 4 tablespoons lemon juice (2 lemons)
- 1 tablespoon finely chopped parsley
- 1 teaspoon dried mint
- 1/2 teaspoon salt (optional)

Instructions:

1. Heat the broth in a 4- or 6-quart pot, on high heat.
2. When the broth boils, add the rice, reduce the heat, cover the pot, and simmer for 15 minutes until the rice is cooked "al dente," firm and not mushy.
3. In a small bowl whisk the eggs until they are frothy. You can use a wire whisk, a rotary beater, or even an electric mixer. Add the lemon juice as you continue whisking. Then take about 1/4 cup (a ladleful) of the hot broth and whisk it into the egg-lemon mixture.
4. Slowly pour the egg-lemon mixture into the soup, while stirring. Cook over low heat for about 3 to 5 minutes, but don't let the soup come to a boil.
5. Ladle the soup into individual bowls, and sprinkle each with a bit of the parsley, the mint, and salt.

Goes well with:

- Drinks: mineral water with a slice of lemon.
- Other recipes: a chicken recipe like Stuffed Chicken Breasts.

Notes/Evaluation:

Nonna's Rice Soup (V)

Special notes:

My mother was a marvelous cook who, like most women of her generation, rarely wrote down recipes, but was willing to tell how she made a dish by indicating "a bit of this" and a "handful of that." This is my interpretation of her recipe. Broth is available in cans or in condensed cubes.

Ingredients:

- 8 cups chicken (or vegetarian) broth
- 2 carrots
- 2 leeks
- 2 celery stalks
- 1 cup rice
- 1 cup grated Parmesan cheese
- 2 egg yolks
- 2 tablespoons water
- 1 tablespoon minced parsley
- 1/2 teaspoon salt

Instructions:

1. Clean the carrots, leeks, and celery; trim each, peel the carrot, and wash under cool running water. Dice all into small pieces.
2. In a large pan (about 6 quarts) place the broth and the diced carrots, leeks, and celery. Heat under medium-high heat for about 20 to 30 minutes. Stir in the rice and cook for 20 minutes.
3. While the rice soup is cooking, in a small bowl mix well the cheese, egg yolks, water, parsley, and salt.
4. When the rice soup is ready (the rice should be firm but cooked), place the cheese and egg mixture in a tureen (soup bowl) and slowly add the soup, mixing well.
5. Serve.

Goes well with:

- Drinks: mineral water, or Sherry.
- Other recipes: crackers, most chicken dishes, a salad.

Notes/Evaluation:

Split Pea Soup

Equipment needed:

cheesecloth and cotton twine (both available at most supermarkets)
colander

Special notes:

This is a very hearty soup, good for cold weather. In Tucson we rarely have either the soup or the cold weather! Ask the butcher for a ham hock, if you don't see it in the meat case.

Ingredients:

- 1 pound green split peas (comes in a package)
- 1/4 cup minced parsley
- 1 teaspoon thyme
- 2 bay leaves
- 1 teaspoon dry rosemary
- 4 cups water
- 1 tablespoon peppercorns
- 1 ham hock (about 1 to 1-1/2 pounds)
- 2 large carrots, peeled and thinly sliced (like dimes)
- 1 onion, coarsely chopped

Instructions:

1. Check the split peas and discard any debris. In a colander rinse well and let drain.
2. Place the parsley, thyme, bay leaves, and rosemary in the middle of a square piece of cheesecloth. Tie the cheesecloth with a piece of cotton twine. You have created what the fancy cookbooks call a "bouquet garni." If you were to add these herbs loosely to the soup, they would be somewhat unsightly and not particularly good to eat once cooked. By placing them in the cheesecloth, you can cook the whole package and remove it once the flavor of these herbs has been added.
3. In a 6-quart pan, combine the beef broth, water, peppercorns, ham hock, and split peas.
4. Use medium-high to low-high heat and bring to a boil. Lower the heat, cover the pot, and let simmer for 1 hour. When you cover the pot, sometimes the contents tend to foam and spill out. To avoid this, place the lid at a slight angle so some of the steam escapes. After a few minutes, when the liquid has settled to a gentle simmer, you can move the lid so it fits squarely.
5. At the end of the hour, add the bouquet garni, the carrots and onion, and continue simmering for another hour.
6. Remove the bouquet garni and discard. Remove the ham hock onto a dish. Pull the meat off the bone, and discard any fat and skin. Cut the meat into bite size pieces, return the meat to the soup, and stir well.

7. Serve and ladle the soup into soup bowls. For an extra touch, warm the soup bowls in the oven before you ladle the soup.

Goes well with:
- Drinks: red wine, sherry.
- Other recipes: this can be a meal in itself, or can be accompanied by a simple salad. Crusty bread goes very well.

Notes/Evaluation:

Stracciatella alla Romana (V)

Special notes:

This is a very popular soup in Italy, served in many restaurants, especially in Rome. As opposed to minestrone, this is a very light broth without any vegetables. The word "stracciare" means to tear or rip into ribbons; the egg mixture that is placed in the broth has this appearance.

Ingredients:

- 8 cups chicken (or vegetable) broth
- 4 eggs, at room temperature
- 1/3 cup freshly grated Parmesan cheese
- 1/2 teaspoon salt
- 1/2 teaspoon white pepper

Instructions:

1. In a saucepan bring the broth to a simmer, using medium to medium-high heat.
2. While the broth is heating, in a bowl beat the eggs with a fork. Add the cheese and stir well.
3. Pour the egg and cheese mixture into the broth and whisk. If necessary increase the heat slightly so the broth is almost at a boiling point. Season with the salt and pepper.
4. Serve with crackers.

Goes well with:

- Drinks: Sherry.
- Other recipes: can be followed by any chicken recipe; a slice of Valerie's cheesecake with peaches would be a superb dessert.

Notes/Evaluation:

Veronica's Mexican Corn Soup

Equipment needed:
electric blender or food processor
3-quart saucepan

Special notes:
A hot and hearty soup.

Ingredients:
- 3 cups fresh (or canned or frozen) corn kernels
- 1 cup chicken broth
- 2 cups milk
- 1/4 cup butter
- 1 garlic clove, minced
- 1 teaspoon oregano
- salt
- freshly ground pepper
- 2 tablespoons diced chilies (4 oz. can)
- 1 boneless chicken breast, cooked and chopped
- 1 cup diced Mexican tomatoes (available in can)
- 1 cup cubed Monterey Jack cheese
- 2 tablespoons minced fresh parsley
- 4 tortillas cut into squares (bite size)

Instructions:
1. Prepare the above ingredients; e.g., mince the garlic, cook the chicken, and chop; dice the tomatoes and cube the cheese; cut the tortillas. To cook the chicken breast, simply heat 1 tablespoon of butter in a pan over medium-high heat, and sauté the chicken for 4 minutes on each side.
2. Combine the corn and the chicken broth in the blender and puree.
3. In a 3-quart saucepan combine the butter and the corn mixture and simmer slowly for 5 minutes; stir well so corn does not stick to bottom of pan.
4. Add milk, garlic, oregano, salt and pepper (to your taste), and bring to boil. Reduce heat, add chilies and simmer 5 minutes.
5. In each serving bowl place some chicken and some tomatoes.
6. Add the cheese to the soup and stir until melted.
7. Ladle the soup into the bowls and sprinkle with parsley and tortilla squares.

Goes well with:
- Drinks: beer, red wine, dry white wine.
- Other recipes: can be a meal in itself; can be accompanied by a salad, or a side dish of sautéed yellow squash.

Notes/Evaluation:

Vichyssoise (Leek and Potato Soup) (V)

Equipment needed:

potato peeler
potato brush
food mill or sieve

Special notes:

This soup is traditionally served cold, but you can serve it either hot or cold. Leeks are part of the onion family and look like large green onions.

Ingredients:

- 3 leeks
- 2 tablespoons butter
- 6 cups chicken (or vegetable) broth
- 4 potatoes
- 1/2 teaspoon salt
- 1/2 teaspoon freshly ground pepper (white if you have it)
- 2 cups heavy cream (only 1/2 cup if you plan to serve this hot)
- 4 teaspoons chopped chives (or the equivalent in finely cut green onions, using the white part only)

Instructions:

1. Clean the leeks by cutting off the root end and most of the green stems. Cut or separate the leeks into individual strips and rinse well under cold water, since they tend to be sandy. Thinly slice the leeks.

2. Scrub the potatoes with a brush under cold running water. Dry them and peel them, cut them into small pieces, about 1/2-inch cubes.

3. In a 6-quart pot melt the butter over medium to medium-high heat. Add the leeks and cook for about 3 minutes, stirring occasionally.

4. Add the broth and the potatoes to the pot and bring to a boil.

5. Simmer for about 15 minutes, until the potatoes are tender.

6. Now comes the tricky part. Place a sieve or a food mill over another large pot (or bowl) and ladle the soup into it a bit at a time, forcing the soup through it.

7. When you are finished, add the salt and pepper, and 1/2 cup of the heavy cream, stir over low to medium heat until the soup simmers. If you plan to serve the soup hot, go ahead and ladle it into soup bowls, or a soup tureen. Garnish with the chopped chives.

8. If you plan to serve the soup cold, add all 2 cups of heavy cream, and stir well. Then chill the soup, and serve it when it is very cold. For an elegant touch chill the soup bowls as well by placing them in the refrigerator a couple of hours before dinner. Garnish the soup with the chives.

Goes well with:

- Drinks: mineral water.
- Other recipes: if this soup is served cold, it could be followed by several appetizers; otherwise a chicken dish like "Pollo alla Cacciatora" would be a nice contrast.

Notes/Evaluation:

Winter Vegetable Soup (V)

Special notes:

As with most soups, you can experiment with a number of the ingredients. For example, if you don't like broccoli you can use other vegetables, like spinach or corn or whatever. You can also use different spices or condiments like Tabasco sauce, basil, marjoram, thyme, etc.

Ingredients:

- 2 tablespoons olive oil
- 2 tablespoons butter
- 1 medium onion, chopped
- 3 garlic cloves, minced
- 2 large cans (49-1/2 ounces) of chicken (or vegetable) broth
- 5 potatoes, cut into bite size
- 1/2 head cauliflower, cleaned and cut into bite size pieces
- 1/2 head broccoli, cleaned and cut into bite size pieces
- 4 carrots
- 1 can stewed tomatoes
- 1 small can peas
- 2 tablespoons Worcestershire sauce
- 2 bay leaves
- 1 teaspoon dry oregano
- 1/2 teaspoon salt
- 1/2 teaspoon freshly ground pepper
- 2 tablespoons chopped fresh parsley

Instructions:

1. Melt the olive oil and butter in a large (6- or 8-quart) pan, over low to medium heat. Add the onion and sauté for about 8 to 10 minutes. Add the garlic, stir and cook for about 5 minutes. Add the broth and the potatoes, increase the heat to medium, and simmer for 15 minutes.
2. Add the other vegetables and simmer for another 15 minutes. I like my vegetables on the crunchy side; if you prefer them softer, simmer longer, and taste test for readiness.
3. Season with salt and pepper, add parsley, and serve with crusty bread.

Goes well with:

- Drinks: red wine (a nice Italian Primitivo – i.e., Zinfandel).
- Other recipes: this is a meal in itself, but could be followed by a salad, and/or a chicken or meat dish.

Notes/Evaluation:

Chicken

Barbecued Chicken with Lemon Sauce

Equipment needed:

barbecue
pastry brush

Special notes:

Have a spray bottle filled with water at the ready to handle flare-ups on the grill.

Ingredients:

- 10 to 12 pieces of chicken
- 1/2 stick of margarine
- 1/2 cup vegetable (corn) oil
- 6 garlic cloves, minced
- 2 tablespoons parsley, minced
- juice from 1 or 2 lemons
- salt & pepper to taste

Instructions:

1. Spray your barbecue grill with cooking oil spray. Preheat the grill.
2. In a saucepan, over low heat, melt the margarine. Add the corn oil and the garlic, mix well. and heat for about 5 minutes. Remove from heat and add the lemon juice, salt, and pepper.
3. On the preheated barbecue grill, using low to medium heat, place the chicken for 5 minutes, then, with a pastry brush, paint each chicken piece with the lemon sauce. Do so every 5 to 10 minutes, and cook for a total of about 45 minutes, until the chicken is well done and not pink on the inside (cut one piece to inspect).

Goes well with:

- Drinks: beer; red or white wine.
- Other recipes: rice, mixed vegetables, salad, French bread.

Notes/Evaluation:

Caribbean Style Chicken

Equipment needed:

large roasting pan, preferably with non-stick surface
cheese grater

Special notes:

Chicken is so versatile and can be prepared in countless ways. The lime flavor in this recipe is quite distinctive. For a nice decorative touch, use an extra lime, slice it, and use the slices to artistically decorate the serving platter.

Ingredients:

- 1 chicken, cut up
- 3 to 4 limes, grate the peel and squeeze the juice
- 1/4 cup regular flour (all purpose)
- 1 teaspoon salt
- 1 teaspoon freshly ground pepper
- 3 tablespoons butter
- 1 can chicken broth (or made from a bouillon cube)
- 2 tablespoons light brown sugar

Instructions:

1. Clean the chicken pieces under the water faucet. Discard any pieces you would not serve (e.g., the neck, etc.). Burn off any hairs there might be, with a match or over a gas flame. Pat dry and place in a bowl.
2. Toss well with the lime juice.
3. Mix the flour, salt, and pepper and coat each piece of chicken with this mixture (use a flat dish).
4. Preheat the oven to 400 degrees.
5. Place the chicken pieces in a large roasting pan (preferably with a non-stick surface). While the oven is preheating, melt the butter in a small pan, over medium heat. When the butter is melted, drizzle each chicken piece with the butter.
6. Mix the broth, grated lime peel, and brown sugar, and pour over the chicken.
7. Bake the chicken in the oven, uncovered, for 45 to 55 minutes, until the chicken is no longer pink. Baste occasionally (3 or 4 times) with the pan juices.
8. When ready, place the chicken pieces on a platter and spoon the pan juices over it (avoid the surface fat).

Goes well with:

- Drinks: margaritas before dinner; white wine like Riesling during dinner.
- Other recipes: rice, salad, French bread.

Notes/Evaluation:

Chicken in White Wine

Equipment needed:

large pan
slotted spoon

Special notes:

Most, if not all, of the alcohol in the wine evaporates with the cooking, so this is a safe recipe for children and pregnant women. The instructions seem a bit long, but it really is easy to prepare.

Ingredients:

- 8 to 12 pieces of chicken
- 1/2 teaspoon of salt

- 4 carrots
- 1/2 teaspoon of salt

- 5 slices of bacon, chopped
- 2 tablespoons butter
- 1/4 cup green onions, minced
- 1 can small white onions (you can use 12 fresh small onions, but they are difficult to peel)
- 2 cups dry white wine (use a jug wine like a Gallo)
- 12 mushroom caps (remove the stems – keep the caps)
- 2 tablespoons white (all purpose) flour

Instructions:

1. Wash the chicken pieces under cold running water. Pat dry with paper towels. Burn off any hairs. Discard any pieces you would not eat (like the neck, etc.). Sprinkle the chicken with salt and set aside.

2. Clean the carrots (wash under cold water and peel away the outer layer). Cook them in boiling salted water for 5 minutes; drain and set aside. Slice thinly.

3. Fry the bacon in a large pan, over medium heat, until it is crisp; remove with slotted spoon and set aside on paper towels.

4. Throw out all of the bacon fat in the pan (use an empty can), except for about 2 teaspoons. Melt the butter in the pan, and add the chicken pieces to brown. Cook for about 10 minutes, turning the chicken frequently.

5. Add the carrot slices, green onions, white onions, and wine to the chicken. Simmer over low to medium heat, covered, for about 30 minutes. Stir every 5 or so minutes, and check that it is simmering rather than burning.

6. Clean the mushroom caps by wiping them with a damp towel. Remove the stems by twisting off, and discard. Add the caps to the pan and simmer for 5 more minutes.

7. Take a large baking pan (9 X 12 inches or larger) and, using the slotted spoon, place the chicken pieces and the vegetables pieces in it; set aside.

8. In a small bowl place the 2 tablespoons of flour, add some of the pan juice, and stir to make a paste. When the paste is well mixed (almost like toothpaste), place the paste back into the pan with the juice, and cook over medium heat for 5 minutes, stirring constantly.

9. Sprinkle the bacon and the paste-juice over the chicken. At this point you could refrigerate the chicken (covered with foil) until you are ready to prepare it for serving.

10. Finally, place the pan with the chicken (foil removed) in the oven at 400 to 450 degrees for about 1 hour; stir occasionally. To serve, place on serving dish and spoon the liquid drippings over the chicken.

Goes well with:

- Drinks: red or white wine (a Pinot Grigio, for example).
- Other recipes: this is a meal in itself, but could be accompanied by a salad or a serving of couscous (comes in a package, follow directions).

Notes/Evaluation:

Chicken Marsala

Equipment needed:

large skillet

Special notes:

Marsala is a wine, somewhat like Vermouth, and like Vermouth it comes in sweet and dry varieties. For this recipe use dry Marsala (if you cannot find Marsala, use dry sherry or dry Vermouth).

Ingredients:

- 4 whole deboned chicken breasts, cleaned, pat dry, cut in half
- 1/4 cup flour
- 1/2 teaspoon salt
- 1/2 teaspoon freshly ground pepper
- 1 tablespoon butter
- 2 tablespoons olive oil
- 1/2 cup dry Marsala
- 1/2 cup chicken broth (from can or cube)

Instructions:

1. Make a mixture of the flour, salt, and pepper on a dish, and dredge the chicken breasts in this mixture, so that they are covered with it.
2. In a large skillet melt the butter and olive oil over medium heat, and brown the chicken breasts on both sides – about 3 to 5 minutes per side.
3. Place the chicken breasts on a platter. Cover with foil to keep warm.
4. In the skillet, add the Marsala and the chicken broth, and bring to a boil. Cook for 3 to 5 minutes to reduce the liquid.
5. Return the chicken breasts to the skillet and heat through, spooning the sauce over the chicken (about 1 or 2 minutes).
6. Serve on a serving platter.

Goes well with:

- Drinks: red or white (dry) wine. Don't use Marsala – it's too desserty.
- Other recipes: rice, salad, mixed vegetables.

Notes/Evaluation:

Chicken Moroccan Style

Equipment needed:

cotton string

Special notes:

This is a wonderful aromatic chicken, with many different spices that blend together well.

Ingredients:

- 1 whole chicken, about 3-1/2 pounds
- 1/4 teaspoon salt
- 1/4 teaspoon ground pepper
- 1/2 teaspoon paprika
- 1/2 teaspoon cumin
- 1/2 teaspoon coriander
- 1/2 teaspoon cinnamon
- 1/2 teaspoon cayenne pepper
- 4 garlic cloves, flattened
- 1 lemon, cut in half
- 3 tablespoons olive oil
- 1/2 to 3/4 cup white wine

Instructions:

1. Preheat the oven to 400 degrees.
2. Clean the chicken. Remove any innards and discard. Pat dry.
3. In a small bowl mix all the spices well (salt through cayenne pepper).
4. Rub the chicken with garlic cloves, and place the cloves in the cavity.
5. Squeeze the lemon halves to extract the juice. Place the halves in the body cavity, and brush the chicken with about 1/2 of the lemon juice. You might need to cut the lemon halves into smaller pieces to fit.
6. Rub the chicken with the spice mixture.
7. Tie the legs of the chicken together with the cotton string.
8. In an ovenproof skillet large enough for the chicken, heat the olive oil over medium high heat.
9. Place the chicken in the skillet, add the remaining lemon juice and the wine, and baste the chicken with the liquid.
10. Place the skillet in the oven for approximately 90 minutes. Baste every 15 to 20 minutes. To test if the chicken is done, pierce the thigh – if the juices are clear, then the chicken is done.
11. Serve hot or cold.

Goes well with:

- Drinks: red or white wine, iced tea.
- Other recipes: a salad; crusty bread; accompanying vegetables like eggplant medley or oven roasted potatoes, or plain rice.

Notes/Evaluation:

Chicken Piccata

Equipment needed:
large skillet, electric or for the stove pepper grinder

Special notes:
Goes great with a side order of plain fettucine. Capers are basically the berries of a plant, and can be purchased in small jars in most large groceries (usually in the gourmet section). They have a pungent taste, and go well on pizzas and salads.

Ingredients:
- 6 chicken breasts, boneless and skinless (wash & pat dry)
- 1/2 stick (4 tablespoons) butter
- 2 tablespoons olive oil
- 3 tablespoons all-purpose flour
- 1 teaspoon salt
- 1 teaspoon freshly ground pepper
- 6 thin slices of lemon
- 2 tablespoons capers
- 1/2 cup dry white wine

Instructions:
1. Heat the butter and oil in a large skillet over medium heat. While this heats up, mix the flour with the salt and pepper in a dish. Pat the chicken breasts onto the flour mix so that they are well coated.
2. Cook the chicken in the butter-oil mixture until the breasts are golden brown, turning them once (about 4 to 8 minutes per side).
3. Add the lemon slices, the capers, and the wine, and cook over medium heat.
4. Cook for a few minutes until the wine mixture is slightly thickened.
5. Place the chicken breasts on a serving platter, top each with a lemon slice, and with the sauce and capers from the pan.

Goes well with:
- Drinks: red or white dry wine.
- Other recipes: fettucine (or spaghetti) as a side dish; rice.

Notes/Evaluation:

Chicken Rolls

Equipment needed:
baking dish

Special notes:
Another elegant but simple dish. Prosciutto is an Italian cured ham. If you cannot find it, use ham, especially "honey ham" or similar variation.

Ingredients:
- 4 chicken breasts, deboned, clean and pat dry
- 1/2 teaspoon each of salt, pepper, and garlic powder, well mixed (for variation, you can use garlic salt or lemon salt, or other prepared combinations)
- 4 thin slices of prosciutto
- 4 thin slices of Swiss cheese (or Fontina cheese)
- 1 egg, beat with fork to blend white and yolk
- 1 cup breadcrumbs, plain or seasoned
- 4 tablespoons butter

Instructions:
1. Preheat the oven to 400 degrees.
2. Take each chicken breast and flatten between pieces of waxed paper. Use a mallet, or other available tool like a rolling pill. The resulting slices should be about 1/4 inch thick. Use a double thickness of wax paper, as it will tear quite easily.
3. Season each chicken slice with the salt mixture.
4. Take one slice of prosciutto and one slice of cheese, and roll them together tightly. Place the roll on a chicken breast and roll up tightly. Tuck in the ends, and use toothpicks to keep the little package together. Repeat procedure with each of the other 3 chicken breasts.
5. Place the butter in a small pan and melt over medium heat.
6. As the butter is melting, dip each chicken breast roll into the egg, and roll in the breadcrumbs. Place in the baking pan, and drizzle the melted butter over them.
7. Bake for about 20 minutes, till the chicken is well cooked.

Goes well with:
- Drinks: red or white dry wine; I like Orvieto or Verdicchio Italian white wine.
- Other recipes: salad, French bread, vegetables, rice.

Notes/Evaluation:

Chicken with Artichoke Hearts

Special notes:

Use boneless chicken breasts rather than debone them yourself. Prosciutto (Italian "ham") is now widely available; do buy the imported variety.

Ingredients:

- 8 boneless chicken breasts (wash and pat dry)
- 4 tablespoons all purpose flour
- 1/2 teaspoon salt
- 1/2 teaspoon freshly ground pepper
- 4 tablespoons olive oil
- 4 tablespoons butter
- 2 teaspoons minced garlic
- 1 large (12 oz.) jar marinated artichoke hearts
- 2 cups mushrooms, sliced thin
- 24 pitted black olives (preferably Kalamata)
- 3/4 cup dry white wine
- 2 tablespoons lemon juice (1 lemon)
- 4 slices of prosciutto, cut into matchstick size

Instructions:

1. In a dish mix the flour with the salt and pepper.
2. Heat the olive oil in a large skillet over medium-high heat.
3. Dredge each chicken breast in the flour mix and sauté until golden brown on both sides.
4. Lower the heat and cook the chicken until well done, about 10 to 15 minutes depending on the thickness. (Turn over about halfway).
5. Remove the chicken, place on a dish, and keep warm by covering with aluminum foil.
6. Leave 1 tablespoon of liquid in the skillet. Place the butter, garlic, artichoke hearts, mushrooms, olives, wine, and lemon juice in the skillet. Simmer until everything is warm.
7. Place the chicken in the skillet to reheat – about 5 minutes.
8. Place the chicken and other ingredients on a platter. Add prosciutto as a garnish, and serve.

Goes well with:

- Drinks: either red or white wine; how about a Chianti or a Sangiovese?
- Other recipes: a small salad to accompany the meal; lots of crusty bread.

Notes/Evaluation:

Chicken with Mushrooms

Equipment needed:

egg slicer (to slice mushrooms easily)

Special notes:

Easy to prepare. When you buy the mushrooms, select ones of uniform size, firm to the touch, and not yellow.

Ingredients:

- 1 cut up chicken (about 2 to 3 pounds)
- 1/4 cup vegetable oil
- 2 garlic cloves, minced
- 1/2 cup chopped onion
- 1/4 teaspoon marjoram
- 1/2 teaspoon salt
- 1/2 teaspoon freshly ground black pepper
- 1 cup dry white wine
- juice of 1 lemon
- 1/2 pound mushrooms
- 3 small tomatoes

Instructions:

1. Clean the chicken pieces under cold running water. Pat dry. Remove any hairs by burning them off. Discard any pieces you would not eat (like the neck, the gizzards, etc.).

2. In a large skillet, heat the vegetable oil over medium heat. Brown all the chicken pieces, turning each piece.

3. Add the garlic, onion, and marjoram, and cook until the onion is limp (5 to 10 minutes). Add the salt, pepper, and wine. Cover the skillet and cook over low heat for about 40 minutes, until the chicken is tender and no longer pink.

4. While the chicken is cooking, clean the mushrooms. Simply use a damp paper towel to wipe them clean. Don't let the mushrooms get waterlogged by washing them under running water. With a knife, cut away a little slice of the stem from each mushroom and discard; these end pieces are usually dry and tough. Slice the mushrooms into uniform slices by using the egg slicer.

5. Cut the tomatoes into wedges, and add the mushrooms, tomatoes, and lemon juice to the skillet. Cook, covered, for 5 to 10 minutes. Serve.

Goes well with:

- Drinks: a nice red wine, either light or hearty.
- Other recipes: a salad, crusty bread, a vegetable side dish.

Notes/Evaluation:

Chicken with Mushrooms Two

Equipment needed:

an egg slicer to slice the mushrooms

Special notes:

I happen to like chicken and mushrooms, so here is another version. Be sure to use a large pot (at least 8 quarts) since this recipe generates a lot of liquid. Incidentally, any left over liquid makes a great pasta sauce!

Ingredients:

- 6 tablespoons butter
- 1 chicken, cut into pieces (about 3 pounds)
- 1/2 cup all purpose flour
- 1 cup chopped onion
- 3 garlic cloves, mashed
- 1 pound mushrooms, sliced
- 1 cup vermouth (dry or sweet, or other wine)
- 1 large can of crushed tomatoes
- 2 bay leaves, crumbled
- 1/2 teaspoon thyme
- 1/2 teaspoon dried basil
- 1 teaspoon salt
- 1/2 teaspoon freshly ground pepper

Notes/Evaluation:

Instructions:

1. Wash the chicken under cold water and pat dry. Throw out any innards, or pieces like the neck that you might not eat. To clean the mushrooms wipe each with a damp paper towel; cut and throw out the lower part of the stem. To slice the mushrooms, use an egg slicer.
2. In a large pan heat the butter over medium to medium-high heat.
3. Meanwhile coat the chicken pieces in the flour. You can spread the flour on a dish to do this.
4. Brown the chicken in the skillet, and set aside on a dish
5. If necessary add more butter to the pan, and brown the onion, the garlic, and the mushrooms.
6. Return the chicken to the pan. Add the vermouth, the tomatoes, and the spices.
7. Cover and simmer for about 1 hour.
8. Serve. You can simply bring the pot to the table.

Goes well with:

- Drinks: a robust red wine like Cabernet Sauvignon or Pinot Noir.
- Other recipes: have lots of crusty bread. This is a meal in itself, but you might want to serve some ice cream as dessert.

Chicken with Pea-pods

Equipment needed:

wok

Special notes:

A stir-fry recipe, easy to do. However, be sure to have all your ingredients ready.

Ingredients:

- 4 chicken breasts, skinned, boned, cleaned, and cut into bite size pieces
- 2 tablespoons sherry
- 2 tablespoons soy sauce
- 2 tablespoons cornstarch

- 1/2 cup chicken broth (canned or from a cube)
- 2 tablespoons soy sauce
- 1 tablespoon cornstarch
- 1 teaspoon sugar

- 1 package frozen pea pods
- 1 clove garlic, minced
- 1 teaspoon gingerroot, minced
- 1/2 cup green onions, sliced
- 1/2 cup carrots, sliced matchstick style
- 1 can water chestnuts, drained and sliced
- 2-3 tablespoons peanut or vegetable oil

Instructions:

1. In a bowl combine the chicken, sherry, soy sauce, and cornstarch. Mix well.
2. In a second bowl, combine the broth, the soy sauce, the cornstarch, and the sugar. Mix well.
3. Heat the wok. When hot add the oil (enough to just coat the wok – about 2 tablespoons). Stir in the garlic and ginger (don't let the garlic burn – if it starts to, lift the wok away from the heat).
4. Add the chicken mixture and stir-fry for a few minutes until the chicken is no longer pink.
5. Add the pea-pods, onions, carrots, water chestnuts, and broth mixture, and stir-fry for a couple of minutes. The dish is ready when the vegetables are hot and crisp, not limp.
6. Serve as is, or on a bed of hot rice.

Goes well with:

- Drinks: hot tea, beer.
- Other recipes: rice, and other Chinese foods.

Notes/Evaluation:

Chinese Chicken with Mushrooms (Moo Goo Gai Pan)

Equipment needed:

wok

Special notes:

Stir-frying is a little like lovemaking. The preparation period takes longer, and you better be ready when things start cooking!

Ingredients:

- 3 chicken breasts, washed, deboned, and cut into bite size pieces (about 1 inch)
- 3 tablespoons cornstarch
- 1/2 teaspoon salt
- 1/2 teaspoon black pepper
- 3 slices of gingerroot (found in produce section)
- 2 garlic cloves
- 1 can of mushrooms (8 oz., buttons or pieces)
- 1 package frozen snow peas
- 1 can water chestnuts (4 oz.) (optional)
- 2 stalks of broccoli
- 4 tablespoons of corn oil or peanut oil

Instructions:

1. Peel and mince the gingerroot and the garlic.
2. In a small bowl or dish, combine the cornstarch, salt, and pepper.
3. Let the snow peas thaw somewhat, and throw out any liquid (use a sieve in the sink).
4. Cut the broccoli stalks into bite size pieces – use both the stalk (unless it is very tough) and the flowerettes.
5. Drain the liquid from the mushrooms, but set aside about 1/2 cup of the liquid. Have the water chestnuts ready (slice them if they need it).
6. Heat the wok. When the wok is hot, put the oil in it. Then dredge the chicken pieces in the cornstarch mixture. Save whatever mixture is left over (you will need it in step #9).
7. Put the gingerroot and garlic in the wok and stir fry (if they start to burn, remove them – they will add flavor, but if kept in the wok, the burnt taste will not be pleasant).
8. Add the chicken and stir fry for 2 or 3 minutes.

9. Add the mushrooms, snow peas, chestnuts, and broccoli. Take the mushroom juice, add to whatever is left of the cornstarch mixture, mix, and add to wok. Continue stir-frying until the chicken pieces are well cooked, but the vegetables should be crisp.
10. Serve in a serving dish.

Goes well with:

- Drinks: hot tea; beer.
- Other recipes: rice, especially Chinese fried rice.

Notes/Evaluation:

Chinese Chicken

Equipment needed:
large pan
roasting pan

Special notes:
A fun recipe, particularly with good friends.

Ingredients:
- 1 chicken (dead, washed, and cut into pieces)
- 1/2 teaspoon ground cinnamon
- 1/2 teaspoon ground ginger
- 1 tablespoon brown sugar
- 1/2 teaspoon ground pepper
- 1 tablespoon soy sauce
- 1 tablespoon white vinegar

- 1 package flour tortillas
- 1 jar Chinese plum sauce

- 12 green onions (sliced or slivered)

Instructions:
1. In a large (4- to 6-quart) pan, bring water to a boil.
2. Meanwhile, rinse the pieces of chicken and pat dry. Discard any pieces you would not eat (e.g., the neck, the gizzards, etc.).
3. When the water is boiling, remove the pan from the heat and plunge the chicken in for 1 minute. Remove and pat dry.
4. In a small bowl combine the six ingredients listed above – from cinnamon to vinegar. Mix these well and brush each chicken piece with the mixture. Place the chicken pieces in a bowl and let marinate, covered, in the refrigerator for about 6 hours.
5. Take a large roasting pan, place a rack in it, and place the chicken on the rack. Roast in oven at 400 degrees for 45 minutes, or until the skin is crisp.
6. Cut the tortillas into quarters, wrap the stack in aluminum foil and place in the oven 15 minutes before the chicken is done.
7. To eat, each person should take a slice of tortilla, place some chicken, plum sauce, and green onion, and eat with the hand. It's messy but delicious!

Goes well with:
- Drinks: beer; hot tea.
- Other recipes: Chinese rice.

Notes/Evaluation:

Jerusalem Style Chicken

Equipment needed:
glass (Pyrex) baking pan

Special notes:
Chicken breasts that are already deboned are expensive. You can do the deboning yourself, or you can leave well enough alone and not debone the chicken breasts. Tahini is a sesame seed paste (used in the hummus recipe), available in specialty stores. If you can't find any, toast 1/4 cup of sesame seeds in a frying pan.

Ingredients:
- 4 chicken breasts (preferably deboned)

- 1/4 cup soy sauce
- 3 tablespoons olive oil
- 4 tablespoons tahini
- 1/2 teaspoon ground pepper
- 1 teaspoon ground ginger
- 2 tablespoons brown sugar
- 3 garlic cloves, minced
- 3 green onions, minced

Instructions:
1. Mix all of the above ingredients (except the chicken) in a small bowl to make the marinade.
2. Place the chicken in a glass baking pan, pour the marinade over it, and refrigerate 2 to 4 hours, turning the chicken pieces from time to time.
3. Broil in the oven for approximately 45 minutes, or until ready (when the meat is no longer pink but is a golden white). While broiling, turn the chicken once or twice.
4. If the baking pan is not too messy, you can serve the chicken directly from the pan; otherwise serve from a platter.

Goes well with:
- Drinks: a dry white wine like Chardonnay or Pinot Grigio.
- Other recipes: rice (follow package directions), or rice with sautéed mixed vegetables.

Notes/Evaluation:

Mediterranean Chicken

Special notes:

The almond and raisins give this recipe a Mideastern flavor.

Ingredients:

- 8 or more pieces of chicken (mixed or all breasts)
- 2 tablespoons water
- 1/2 teaspoon turmeric
- 1/2 ground cinnamon
- 1/8 teaspoon ground cloves
- 1/2 teaspoon freshly ground pepper
- 2 tablespoons olive oil
- 1/2 cup chopped onion (about 1/2 to 1 onion)
- 2 garlic cloves minced
- 1 cup orange juice
- 2 tablespoons raisins (dark or golden)
- 12 whole almonds
- 2 tablespoons capers
- 2 tablespoons orange peel, cut to matchstick size

Instructions:

1. Wash the chicken well and drain. Pat dry with paper towels.
2. Combine the next 5 ingredients in a small bowl to make a liquid paste. Brush the paste on the chicken pieces, and set aside.
3. In a large heavy pan heat the olive oil over medium heat.
4. Add the onion and garlic and sauté while stirring.
5. Stir in the orange juice, raisins, almonds, and capers. Add the chicken. Cover and bring to a boil (just a few minutes).
6. Reduce the heat and let the chicken simmer for about 1 to 1-1/2 hours, until the chicken is cooked. From time to time, baste the chicken (cover with) with the juices. About 10 minutes before it is ready, add the orange peel.
7. Place the chicken pieces on a serving platter and spoon the sauce over them.

Goes well with:

- Drinks: a mild red wine like Bardolino or Sangiovese.
- Other recipes: a salad; serve with plenty of crusty bread.

Notes/Evaluation:

Peanut Butter Chicken

Equipment needed:
skillet

Special notes:
Don't turn your nose up at this recipe because it uses peanut butter; it is a wonderfully tasting recipe.

Ingredients:
- 1 chicken, cut up (wash and pat dry)
- 1/3 cup peanut oil
- 2 cups minced onions
- 1/2 cup peanut butter (crunchy or smooth)
- 1/2 teaspoon Cayenne pepper
- 1/2 teaspoon salt
- 2 cups water
- 1/4 cup chopped peanuts

Instructions:
1. Heat the oil in a large skillet, over medium heat. Add the chicken and brown. Cook the chicken until tender (about 30 minutes), turning occasionally. Set chicken aside on a platter.
2. Throw out all of the oil in the skillet except for about 2 tablespoons (be careful with hot oil; I pour mine into an empty coffee can).
3. To the skillet add the onions and cook for about 5 minutes over medium heat.
4. Add the peanut butter, cayenne pepper, salt, and water and mix well.
5. Add the chicken pieces to the skillet, and simmer for 10 to 15 minutes, until the liquid thickens.
6. Place the chicken on a serving platter. Spoon the liquid over it and garnish with the chopped nuts.

Goes well with:
- Drinks: if you feel adventurous you can serve orchata, a rice drink found in many stores (next to the milk); if not, serve with beer or wine.
- Other recipes: salad; side order of vegetables.

Notes/Evaluation:

Pollo alla Cacciatora (Chicken, Hunter Style)

Equipment needed:

large heavy skillet
baking dish
pepper grinder
slotted spoon

Special notes:

A very hearty meal; to slice mushrooms I use an egg slicer.

Ingredients:

- 6 to 8 pieces of chicken
- 1 to 2 pounds Italian sausage links
- 4 large red peppers, cored, seeded, each one cut into 10 to 16 vertical slices
- 1 pound fresh mushrooms (or 8 oz. can) sliced
- 4 cups chicken broth (canned or from cubes)
- 1/2 cup of Marsala (or sweet Vermouth, or Sherry)
- 1/4 cup olive oil
- garlic salt & freshly ground pepper

Instructions:

1. Prepare the peppers and the mushrooms.
2. In a large heavy skillet heat the oil over medium-high heat. Brown the bell peppers, stirring frequently, for about 5 minutes. Using a slotted spoon remove the peppers into a large bowl.
3. Clean the chicken pieces using running cold water. Pat the chicken pieces dry and sprinkle with salt and pepper. Brown the chicken in the skillet until lightly brown – about 10 minutes. Remove from skillet and place in a separate bowl.
4. Brown the sausage pieces in the skillet. If you need to, add more olive oil. Remove sausage from skillet into the first bowl (with the peppers).
5. Now brown the mushrooms. If you use canned mushrooms you'll need less time. Remove the mushrooms, and place them into the first bowl.
6. Now add the chicken broth and the marsala to the skillet, and gently mix the liquid, scraping up any bits in the skillet. Bring to a boil, reduce the heat, and let simmer for about 5 minutes.

7. Preheat the oven to 350 degrees. In a baking dish arrange the chicken in a single layer and top with the sausage, bell peppers, mushrooms, and broth mixture. Cover the baking dish (with aluminum foil if necessary) and cook for approximately one hour, until chicken is tender and not pink (pierce with a fork to assess readiness and color). Baste every ten to fifteen minutes.

8. Transfer the food to a serving platter. Remove surface fat from pan juices using a spoon (just skim the surface). Pour clear juice into a pan and boil until liquid is reduced. Spoon some of the liquid over the chicken and serve. The remaining juice can be served separately (or use as a spaghetti sauce for your next meal).

Goes well with:

- Drinks: a robust red wine, like Burgundy or Chianti.
- Other recipes: French or Italian bread; serve pears and cheese for dessert.

Notes/Evaluation:

Pollo all'aglio (Garlic Chicken)

Equipment needed:

roasting pan
pastry brush

Special notes:

If you like roasted chicken, you'll love this one!

Ingredients:

- 4 tablespoons butter
- 6-8 pieces of chicken
- 6-8 potatoes
- 2 heads of garlic
- 1/4 cup of pancake syrup (maple flavor)
- 4 tablespoons honey
- salt

Instructions:

1. Clean the chicken under running cold water and pat dry.
2. Turn on oven to 400 degrees. Place the butter in a large roasting pan and melt in the oven.
3. While butter is melting, scrub the potatoes clean, dry them with a paper towel, and cut them into bite size pieces. No need to peel them, but remove any unsightly blemishes.
4. Separate the heads of garlic into individual cloves. Do not peel the cloves, but do remove the outer peel (the white part).
5. When the butter is melted, place chicken, potatoes, and garlic in the pan. Mix so they become coated with melted butter. Sprinkle with 1 to 2 teaspoons of salt.
6. Bake for 30 minutes, basting with the pan liquid 3 or 4 times (if you need to, add some more butter).
7. In a small bowl mix the maple syrup, honey, and 1/2 teaspoon salt, and brush the chicken and the potatoes with this mixture.
8. Bake another 20 to 30 minutes, again basting with the pan liquid. Chicken and potatoes are ready when they are fork-tender.
9. Serve on a platter. The garlic cloves can be eaten but without the skin; the garlic can be spread on the chicken or eaten by itself; it will be sweet tasting and without the "bite" of raw garlic.

Goes well with:

- Drinks: red or dry white wine; good choices would be a Merlot or Bardolino for a red, and a Chardonnay for a white.
- Other recipes: this is a meal in itself, but might be accompanied by a side serving of vegetables, such as peas, carrots, etc.

Notes/Evaluation:

Pollo con Riso (Chicken with Rice)

Equipment needed:

oven-proof container, like a roasting pan

Special notes:

You can use other chicken parts besides breasts; saffron is incredibly expensive (but worth it).

Ingredients:

- 1-1/2 cups chicken broth (either in a can or cubes)
- 1/2 teaspoon chili powder
- 1/2 teaspoon saffron
- 4 chicken breasts
- 2 garlic cloves minced
- 2 tablespoons olive oil
- 2 tablespoons butter
- 1 cup rice (uncooked)
- 1 cup dry white wine (like Chablis)
- 1/4 teaspoon pepper
- 1/2 cup (1 can or jar) of olives (green, medium sized, stuffed with pimentos)
- 1/2 teaspoon salt
- 1/2 teaspoon freshly ground pepper

Instructions:

1. Heat the chicken broth and dissolve the chili powder and the saffron in it – do not boil.
2. Preheat the oven to 275 degrees. Clean the chicken breasts under cold running water, and pat dry.
3. In a skillet sauté the garlic in the heated olive oil and butter (heat over medium heat – do not burn).
4. Add the chicken breasts and sauté until golden on both sides.
5. In a heavy, oven-proof container combine the rice, broth, wine, salt, and pepper. Bring the mixture to a boil. Place the chicken breasts on top, add whatever pan juices are left, and bake, covered, in the oven at 275 degrees for 45 to 50 minutes, until the rice is done and the chicken is well cooked.
6. Add the olives and heat for 5 minutes more. Serve.

Goes well with:

- Drinks: dry white wine, like Chablis.
- Other recipes: French bread.

Notes/Evaluation:

Roasted Chicken with Vegetables

Equipment needed:

brush to clean potatoes
peeler for carrots

Special notes:

After you've tried this basic recipe you might want to try variations, by altering and/or omitting some of the ingredients. For example, you don't need to use a whole chicken, but you could use cut up pieces. You could add olives, or use some other vegetables like celery, tomatoes, turnips, white onions, etc.

Ingredients:

- 1 tablespoon dried thyme
- 2 tablespoons dried rosemary
- 1 teaspoon salt
- 1 teaspoon freshly ground pepper

- 4 potatoes
- 4 carrots
- 4 green onions
- 1/2 pound mushrooms

- 1 whole chicken (about 3 to 3-1/2 pounds)
- 3 tablespoons olive oil
- 6 garlic cloves

Instructions:

1. In a small bowl mix the spices together (thyme through pepper).

2. Prepare the vegetables. Scrub the potatoes and quarter them. Place them in a bowl of cold water so they won't discolor. Peel the carrots and cut into chunks about 2 inches long (about the length of a thumb). Cut out the green part and the tendrils of the green onions, and wash them (as you do the outer layer will probably peel off). Clean the mushrooms by wiping with a damp towel. Cut off the lowest portion of the stem.

3. Clean the chicken by discarding the insides and washing well under cold water. Pat dry.

4. Preheat the oven to 350 degrees.

5. Place the chicken in an ovenproof pan; rub the pan with oil or butter first so the chicken won't stick. Rub the chicken with 2 of the garlic cloves; flatten them out first with the flat blade of a knife or your palm. Brush the chicken with one tablespoon of olive oil. Rub the chicken with about 1/2 of the spice mixture.

6. Add the vegetables to the pan. Add all the garlic cloves (even the two you used). Sprinkle with the remaining olive oil (3 tablespoons) and the remaining spice mixture.

7. Cook in the oven for about 80 minutes, turning the vegetables every 20 minutes or so, till the chicken is well cooked. Pierce the thigh – if the juices run clear, it is ready. Check also that the potatoes are well done, tender but not mushy.
8. When the chicken is ready, place on a serving platter. Have a sharp knife to cut the chicken.

Goes well with:

- Drinks: a hearty red wine like Cabernet Sauvignon.
- Other recipes: this is a meal in itself, particularly if served with lots of crusty bread. If you like, a small salad or a light dessert (like ice cream or frozen yogurt) would go well.

Notes/Evaluation:

Stir-fried Chicken and Vegetables

Equipment needed:

wok

Special notes:

Deboning chicken consists of removing, with a sharp knife, the skin, fat, and bones of the chicken, with as little damage to yourself as possible. If you don't like the sight of blood (especially your own), you might consider buying chicken breasts that are already deboned (though they are more expensive).

Ingredients:

For marinade:

- 4 tablespoons soy sauce
- 2 tablespoons Sherry
- 2 teaspoons cornstarch
- 1/2 teaspoon sugar
- 1/2 teaspoon granulated ginger (found in spice section of store)
- 1/4 teaspoon garlic powder
- 4 chicken breasts, deboned and cut into bite size pieces
- 1 cup rice
- 4 green onions, slice white part thinly, discard green part
- 1 pound mushrooms, sliced (fresh or canned)
- 1 cup frozen peas (follow package directions to thaw)
- 1 to 4 tablespoons peanut oil or vegetable oil

Instructions:

1. In a small bowl mix well the first six ingredients (from soy sauce through garlic powder) to make a marinade.
2. Pour the marinade over the chicken pieces, mix well, and place in refrigerator for at least one hour.
3. Cook the rice, following the directions on the package.
4. Heat the work. When hot, add 1 or 2 tablespoons of oil. Swirl the oil around so the surface of the wok is covered. Add the onions, mushrooms, and peas. Cook and stir for several minutes, so the vegetables are crisp (not mushy).
5. Remove the vegetables to a bowl and keep warm by covering bowl with a lid, or foil.
6. Add another 1 or 2 tablespoons oil to wok and swirl. Add the chicken pieces and stir frequently. When the chicken is tender and no longer pink, add the vegetables, and stir for a minute or two.
7. Serve with the rice, either separately or mixed.

Goes well with:

- Drinks: tea, beer.
- Other recipes: other Chinese food (e.g. a package of prepared spring rolls or potstickers).

Stir-fried Chicken Cashew

Equipment needed:

wok
several bowls

Special notes:

Stir-frying is a very fast procedure, so you need to have all the ingredients prepared and at your elbow.

Ingredients:

- 1 teaspoon corn starch
- 1 dash of Tabasco
- 1 teaspoon sugar
- 1 tablespoon white wine vinegar
- 1 tablespoon soy sauce

- 3 to 4 chicken breasts, deboned and cut into bite size pieces
- 2 tablespoons soy sauce
- 1 tablespoon cornstarch

- 3 tablespoons peanut oil or vegetable oil
- 1/4 cup salted cashews (or other nuts like walnuts)
- 2 bell peppers, cut into bite size pieces
- 1 onion, cut into 8 wedges
- 1/4 teaspoon minced ginger (fresh or from spice container)

Instructions:

1. First prepare all the ingredients. In a bowl mix the first five ingredients and set aside.
2. In a second bowl, mix two tablespoons soy sauce and 1 of cornstarch, add the chicken pieces, and mix.
3. Place the bell pepper pieces into a third bowl (discard seeds, stem, and any white parts), and add the onion wedges, and the minced ginger.
4. Now heat the wok over medium-high heat. When hot, add 2 tablespoons oil. Add nuts and stir for one minute, till the nuts are browned (don't let them burn – you might want to lower the heat a bit). Remove the nuts with a slotted spoon and set aside.
5. Add chicken to wok and stir-fry for 3 to 4 minutes until no longer pink. Return chicken to bowl.
6. Add 1 tablespoon oil to wok and add contents of third bowl (bell peppers and onions). Stir-fry for about 4 minutes, till vegetables are crisp. Add chicken pieces and cooking sauce (bowl #1) to wok, and stir-fry for about a minute. Stir in cashews. Remove from heat and place on serving dish.

Goes well with:

- Drinks: hot tea.
- Other recipes: rice, other Chinese food like egg rolls.

Notes/Evaluation:

CHICKEN

Stuffed Chicken Breasts

Equipment needed:

heavy frying pan or skillet
pepper grinder

Special notes:

There are many variations of this recipe; it is a good one to experiment with, by varying ingredients.

Ingredients:

- 4 chicken breasts, deboned, and halved
- 1/2 teaspoon salt
- 1/4 teaspoon freshly ground pepper
- 8 pieces of butter, each about 1/2 of a tablespoon
- 3 tablespoons parsley, minced
- 2 tablespoons chives
- 2 garlic cloves, finely minced

- 1/4 cup white flour
- dash cayenne pepper
- 1 egg, beaten, with 2 tablespoons of water
- 1/2 cup or more of olive oil
- 1/2 pound mushrooms, sliced
- 2 tablespoons butter
- 1/2 cup dry white wine (like a Chablis)

Instructions:

1. Take each half of chicken breast and pound between sheets of waxed paper, using a mallet or a rolling pin, to a thickness of about 1/4 inch. Sprinkle both sides of each piece with salt and pepper.

2. In the middle of each chicken slice place two pieces of butter. Mix the parsley, chives, and garlic, and sprinkle over the chicken only on the butter side.

3. Roll up the chicken breasts, securing with toothpicks.

4. Mix the flour with the cayenne in a dish. Coat each chicken roll with flour, then with egg, and then with breadcrumbs.

5. Heat the oil in a heavy frying pan over medium to medium high heat. Fry the chicken rolls in the hot oil until they are brown on all sides (about 5 to 7 minutes). Place on a dish with a paper towel to absorb some of the oil, and keep warm (cover with foil).

6. Sauté the mushrooms in the butter over medium to high medium heat. Stir in the white wine and increase the heat. Keep stirring till the liquid is reduced to half its volume.

7. Place the chicken on a serving dish and pour the mushrooms and liquid over them.

Goes well with:
- Drinks: red wine.
- Other recipes: salad, French bread, vegetables, rice.

Notes/Evaluation:

Meat

Barbecue Tomato Sauce (Salsa)

Equipment needed:
food processor (or sharp knife)

Special notes:
This is a good sauce to spoon over barbecued steaks, or to use as a dipping "salsa" for tortilla chips. Cumin is usually available in the spice section of your grocery store.

Ingredients:
- 6 tomatoes, preferably somewhat ripe
- 3 onions, white or yellow
- 1 can green chilies (small – 4 oz.)
- 2 tablespoons red wine vinegar
- 1/4 cup olive oil
- 1/4 teaspoon oregano (dry)
- 1/2 teaspoon cumin
- garlic salt or plain salt to taste

Instructions:
1. Mince the first three ingredients, using a knife or kitchen food processor (do not use a blender – it will liquefy the ingredients too much).
2. Place the ingredients in a large bowl. Add the remaining ingredients and mix well.
3. Let sit in the refrigerator several hours so flavors blend well. If possible, serve at room temperature.

Goes well with:
- Drinks: beer, especially Mexican like La Corona, Double XX, or Negra Modelo.
- Other recipes: goes well on steaks, hamburgers, tacos, or as a dip.

Notes/Evaluation:

Barbecued Sirloin Steaks a la Bourbon

Equipment needed:

glass or ceramic bowl

Special notes:

Other alcoholic liquids (such as white wine, vermouth, etc.) may be used. During grilling the alcohol evaporates and leaves the fragrances behind to flavor the meat.

Ingredients:

- 4 top sirloin steaks (or T-bone steaks or any other cut of meat you favor)
- 1 cup bourbon (better taste to make sure it's fresh…)
- salt and pepper
- cooking oil spray

Instructions:

1. Place the steaks in a glass or ceramic bowl. Sprinkle with the bourbon, salt, and pepper.
2. Let stand at room temperature for about 2 hours, turning at least once.
3. Barbecue, about 3 to 9 minutes per side, depending on thickness of meat, and how well done you wish the meat to be. Do spray your barbecue rack with cooking oil spray, so the meat doesn't stick.

Goes well with:

- Drinks: a hearty red wine like a Pinot Noir.
- Other recipes: baked potato, corn on the cob, grilled vegetables, salad.

Notes/Evaluation:

Beef a la Bourguignonne

Special notes:

For best results follow step number 1 to marinate the meat overnight. Otherwise, simply add the wine to the meat and continue with instructions. This is really a stew and great in cold weather.

Ingredients:

- 4 pounds meat (you can use top round, beef chuck, bottom round roast, or other meat) cut into cubes about 1-1/2 to 2 inches
- 3 cups red wine (like a burgundy)
- 1/2 cup olive oil
- 1 onion, minced
- 2 cloves of garlic, minced
- 1 bay leaf
- 2 tablespoons chopped parsley
- 1/2 teaspoon thyme
- 2 cups beef broth (can or cubes)
- 1 teaspoon white pepper
- 1 teaspoon salt
- 4 carrots, peeled and cut into 1/2-inch pieces
- 8 ounces button mushrooms
- 12 pitted olives (green or black)

Instructions:

1. Place the cubes of meat in a large bowl and add the wine. Mix well and let it marinate overnight, in the refrigerator. You might want to cover the bowl with plastic wrap so it doesn't pick up other refrigerator flavors.
2. Heat the oil in a large pot (6 or 8 quarts), using medium to medium high heat, and brown the meat in it. You might need to do this in batches. Temporarily remove the meat to a platter or bowl.
3. Add the onion and garlic to the pot, and sauté till golden brown.
4. Return the meat to the pot and add the other ingredients except for the carrots and mushrooms. Stir well, reduce the heat to low, cover the pot, and cook for about 2 hours, stirring occasionally.
5. Clean the mushrooms by wiping them gently with a damp paper towel. Slice off the bottom portion of the stem (about the thickness of a dime) and discard.
6. Add the carrots and the mushrooms to the pot, stir gently, and cook covered for another 20-30 minutes, until they are tender.
7. About 5 or 10 minutes before serving, add the olives.

8. Serve. If this is an informal occasion, simply serve from the pot. If it is a more special occasion, use a soup tureen or other suitable container.

Goes well with:

- Drinks: the same red wine you used.
- Other recipes: this is a full meal in itself. Serve with lots of crusty bread.

Notes/Evaluation:

Chili con Carne

Equipment needed:

wooden spoon

Special notes:

This is a standard Mexican recipe, with probably hundred of variations. It is one of those recipes you can experiment with by changing the proportion of various ingredients, or adding others. When you seed and mince the jalapeno peppers, don't touch them with your bare hands as they might burn (though most store-bought jalapenos aren't very hot). To be safe, do use gloves (or plastic bags).

Ingredients:

- 2 tablespoons olive oil
- 2 pounds lean ground beef
- 2 large onions, minced
- 6 garlic cloves, minced
- 1 28-oz. can plum tomatoes (or stewed tomatoes)
- 3-4 fresh jalapeno peppers, seeded and minced
- 6 tablespoons chili powder
- 1 tablespoon paprika
- 1 teaspoon cumin
- 1 can (or bottle) beer

Instructions:

1. Heat the oil in a 6-quart pan, over medium-high heat.
2. Add the ground beef, onions, and garlic, and sauté till the meat is browned, while stirring with a wooden spoon.
3. Add all the other ingredients, mix well, and bring to a boil. Reduce the heat to medium-low.
4. Simmer uncovered about 50 to 60 minutes, stirring occasionally, until the meat is tender and the liquid has thickened.

Goes well with:

- Drinks: cold beer.
- Other recipes: salad; a side order of refried beans (follow directions on the can); tortillas as bread.

Notes/Evaluation:

London Broil

Equipment needed:
electric knife (optional)

Special notes:
Flank steak, a somewhat tougher cut of meat, is traditionally used for this recipe. The meat is cooked as one piece and then thinly sliced against the grain before it is served. You can make steak sandwiches, or serve with crusty bread.

Ingredients:
- 1-1/2 pounds of flank steak (one piece)
- 1 tablespoon garlic salt
- 1 teaspoon dried oregano
- olive oil or oil spray (to oil the pan)
- Worcestershire sauce (optional)

Instructions:
1. With a sharp knife score the meat on both sides using a diamond pattern. The cuts should be about 1/4 inch deep. This will "tenderize" the meat.
2. Rub the meat well with the three other ingredients (if you want to, you can mix the ingredients in a small dish before the rub).
3. With a little bit of olive oil or oil spray, cover the surface of a large griddle or heavy skillet (the oil is so the meat won't stick).
4. Heat the skillet over high heat. When the skillet is hot, broil the steak about 5 or 6 minutes on each side (do not overcook as London Broil becomes tough).
5. Remove the steak from the skillet, place on a cutting board (or platter) and let it sit for about 5 minutes.
6. Slice into thin slices, about 1/4 inch thick, across the grain (an electric knife makes the job easier), and serve. I like to add a few splashes of Worcestershire sauce.

Goes well with:
- Drinks: a hearty red wine like Cabernet Sauvignon.
- Other recipes: a small salad; a simple vegetable like carrots; lots of crusty bread.

Notes/Evaluation:

Pepper Steak (Steak au Poivre)

Special notes:

Peppercorns are simply whole cloves of pepper before they are ground. They can be found in most supermarkets in the spice section. Beef cubes for broth can also be purchased in most supermarkets, in small jars.

Ingredients:

- 4 steaks cut about 3/4-inch thick (you can use top round, sirloin, strip steaks,etc.) preferably boneless
- 4 tablespoons cracked green (or black) peppercorns
- 2 tablespoons butter
- 4 tablespoons finely chopped shallots (or onions)
- 4 tablespoons brandy
- 1 cup beef broth (in a container or from cubes)

Instructions:

1. Rub or press the peppercorns into the meat, all sides. Chill the meat for about 1 hour.
2. In a large frying pan melt the butter over high heat (but don't let it burn).
3. Add the steaks and sear for 6 to 7 minutes each side. If your pan is not large enough to handle four steaks, either do them in batches or have two pans going at the same time.
4. Remove the steaks to a hot platter and cover with aluminum foil. (You can warm the platter in the oven at a low setting.)
5. In the pan, over medium high heat, add the shallots and sauté till golden.
6. Add the brandy carefully and let it flame. Add the beef broth and bring it to a boil. Let it evaporate till you have about half the original liquid left (about 7 to 10 minutes).
7. Spoon the sauce over the meat and serve. (For a colorful flourish, take another two tablespoons of brandy, warm in a metal ladle, light and, while it is flaming, spoon over the steaks at the table. (Make sure your fire insurance policy is paid up!)

Goes well with:

- Drinks: any red wine (if you've never tried an Italian "Dolcetto d'Alba," this might be the time to do it).
- Other recipes: a simple side of vegetables; crusty bread; a salad.

Notes/Evaluation:

Pork Chops in White Wine

Equipment needed:

skillet
egg slicer
pepper grinder

Special notes:

This is a "safe" recipe for children, since the alcohol in the wine will burn off. Use an egg slicer to slice the fresh mushrooms.

Ingredients:

- 4 pork chops
- 1 can of mushrooms (or 1/2 pound fresh)
- 2 tomatoes, diced
- 3 tablespoons olive oil
- 1 onion, minced
- 1 garlic clove, minced
- 1 cup dry white wine (like Chablis or Riesling)
- 1/2 cup of water
- 1/2 teaspoon fresh basil, minced
- 1/2 teaspoon rosemary (dry or fresh), minced
- 1/2 teaspoon salt
- 1/2 teaspoon pepper
- 1 tablespoon minced fresh parsley

Instructions:

1. Heat the olive oil in the skillet. If using fresh mushrooms, clean them, slice them, and add the mushrooms, onion, and garlic to the skillet, and stir for about 5 minutes (if using canned mushrooms, add them in step 6).
2. Remove the mushrooms to a small bowl.
3. In the skillet over medium high heat, cook the pork chops until they are browned, on both sides. If necessary add some more olive oil. Add the wine, water, and spices.
4. Bring to a boil, stirring the liquid and scraping the brown bits from the sides and bottom of the skillet.
5. Reduce heat to low, cover the skillet, and simmer for 45 minutes.
6. Add the mushrooms and the tomatoes to the skillet, stir and cook for 15 more minutes till the vegetables are heated.
7. Sprinkle pork chops with parsley and serve.

Goes well with:

- Drinks: the rest of the white wine you use.
- Other recipes: a salad and some French bread.

Notes/Evaluation:

Pork Fajitas

Equipment needed:

glass or ceramic bowl
skillet

Special notes:

Fajitas can be made with any cut of meat, and quite often the recipe specifies chicken or beef.

Ingredients:

- 3 tablespoons Worcestershire sauce
- 3 tablespoons wine vinegar
- 2 tablespoons water
- 1/2 teaspoon salt
- 4 garlic cloves, minced
- 4 small to medium size pork cutlets
- 1/4 cup minced onion
- 4 tomatoes, minced
- 1 green bell pepper, cut into matchstick size
- 4 tablespoons Mexican salsa
- 1/2 teaspoon freshly ground black pepper
- 4-8 tortillas
- 1/2 cup sour cream

Instructions:

1. In a skillet combine the Worcestershire sauce, vinegar, water, salt, and 1/2 of the minced garlic; cook and stir over medium heat for 2 to 4 minutes, until the mixture is heated.
2. Place the cutlets in a glass (or ceramic) bowl and pour the mixture over them, coating each cutlet well. Set aside for at least 15 to 30 minutes, to marinate.
3. In a separate bowl, combine the onion, tomatoes, bell pepper, salsa, black pepper, and the remaining minced garlic. Stir well and refrigerate for at least 30 minutes.
4. Remove the cutlets from the marinade and broil them, basting with the marinade, and turning several times. Cook until the cutlets are browned on the outside and no longer pink on the inside (at least 10 minutes).
5. While the pork cutlets are broiling, heat the vegetable mixture in a pan and warm the tortillas on a hot griddle or similar surface – even a non-stick pan over low heat (don't let those cutlets burn!).
6. When the cutlets are cooked, place them on a cutting board and slice thinly.

7. Mix the pork and the vegetable mixture and serve with the warm tortillas. Spoon sour cream on top.

Goes well with:

- Drinks: beer, especially Mexican beer, or margaritas.
- Other recipes: salsa with chips.

Notes/Evaluation:

Pork Medallions with Mustard-cream Sauce

Equipment needed:

a meat pounder (looks like a hammer or mallet)

Special notes:

This is somewhat similar to "Cotolette alla Milanese" (cutlets Milan style), a well known dish. When you serve this on a platter, decorate it with cherry tomatoes or sprigs of parsley, for a special touch of elegance.

Ingredients:

- 4 green onions
- 6 boneless pork cutlets
- 1/3 cup all purpose flour
- 1/2 teaspoon salt
- 1/2 teaspoon freshly ground pepper
- 4 tablespoons butter
- 1/3 cup dry white wine (like Chardonnay or Riesling)
- 1 cup whipping cream
- 4 tablespoons Dijon style mustard

Instructions:

1. Clean the green onions by trimming the tendrils (root-like part). Wash under cold running water, and discard the outer layer which will come apart anyway. Slice the onions into dime-thin slices, but keep the white and green portions separate.
2. Pound the pork cutlets between sheets of waxed paper to about 1/4-inch thickness. You can use the flat portion of a meat pounder, or the bottom of a solid jar (but be careful).
3. In a flat dish mix the flour, salt, and pepper.
4. Melt one tablespoon of butter in a heavy large skillet, over medium to medium high heat. Take 2 of the pork cutlets, dredge them on both sides in the mixed flour, and shake off the excess.
5. Saute the cutlets until they are brown and cooked through – about 3 to 5 minutes per side. Transfer the cutlets to a platter and cover with aluminum foil to keep warm. Repeat the procedure with the other cutlets, melting 1 tablespoon of butter each time.

6. After the last cutlets are removed from the skillet, add the white part of the minced green onions to the skillet, and sauté for 2 minutes. Stir in the white wine and boil until the liquid is reduced to about 2 tablespoons – this should take about 3 to 5 minutes.

7. Add the whipping cream and the mustard and simmer until the liquid is thickened to the consistency of a sauce – about 5 to 7 minutes. Stir occasionally.

8. Season the sauce with salt and pepper – more or less to your taste.

9. Spoon the sauce over the pork cutlets and sprinkle the green part of the green onions as a garnish. Serve.

Goes well with:

- Drinks: red wine, even a Beaujolais.
- Other recipes: excellent with oven roasted potatoes, or peas.

Notes/Evaluation:

Pork Roast, Piemonte Style

Equipment needed:

roasting pan with a rack in it
cotton string (kite string will do)

Special notes:

Piemonte is a region in northern Italy. The original recipe calls for pancetta rather than bacon, but unless you live in a large city with good Italian delis (like New York), you'll have to use bacon.

Ingredients:

- 2 tablespoons olive oil
- 2 teaspoons dry rosemary
- 2 teaspoons dry sage
- 2 cloves garlic, minced
- 1/2 teaspoon garlic salt
- 1/2 teaspoon freshly ground pepper
- 4 pound pork loin roast (with or without bones)
- 6 slices bacon

Instructions:

1. In a small bowl mix the olive oil, rosemary, sage, garlic, garlic salt, and pepper (with both the rosemary and the sage, crush the herbs between thumb and finger before placing in bowl, so as to release the aromatic oils).
2. Brush or rub the herb mixture all over the roast.
3. Place about four cotton strings (about 18 inches long) across a rack in a roasting pan. Place the roast on the rack, and lay the six slices of bacon across the top of the roast. Tie the strings so they keep the roast and the bacon strips together. Sprinkle a bit more of the rosemary and sage on top of the bacon.
4. Roast pork for 1-1/2 to 2 hours at 325 Degrees. Make sure the pork is done (meat should not be pink).
5. Place roast on a serving platter or carving board. Remove the strings. Keep the roast warm, but let it sit for about 10 minutes before slicing.

Goes well with:

- Drinks: a light or hearty red wine, like a Gamay or a Burgundy.
- Other recipes: a salad, a side dish of vegetables, especially roasted potatoes.

Notes/Evaluation:

Rib Eye Roast

Equipment needed:
roasting pan with a rack inside it
pepper grinder

Special notes:
You will have leftover meat, which is delicious cold, or sliced thin for sandwiches.

Ingredients:
- 4 pound rib eye roast (with or without bones)
- 1 teaspoon salt
- 1/2 teaspoon thyme
- 1/2 teaspoon freshly ground pepper

Instructions:
1. Preheat the oven to 350 degrees. While the oven is preheating, combine the salt, thyme, and pepper in a small dish and rub the roast with this mixture.
2. Place a rack in the roasting pan, and place the roast, fat side up, on the rack. Cook in the oven for about 20 to 25 minutes per pound (a 4-pound roast requires about 90 minutes or more, depending on how well done you like it).
3. When the roast is ready, place on a serving platter, let stand for 15 minutes, and slice if there is no bone, or carve if there is one.

Goes well with:
- Drinks: red wine, like a Barolo or a Shiraz.
- Other recipes: potatoes, or other vegetable, French bread.

Notes/Evaluation:

Steak with Cognac Sauce

Equipment needed:

heavy skillet or electric frying pan

Special notes:

A very elegant serving

Ingredients:

- 4 small boneless rib-eye (or similar) steaks
- 1/2 cup of beef broth (canned or from cubes)
- 1 teaspoon Dijon style mustard (Grey Poupon, of course!)
- 2 teaspoons Worcestershire sauce
- 1 teaspoon lemon juice
- 2 teaspoons cream Sherry
- 2 teaspoons Cognac (or Brandy)
- 1/2 teaspoon cornstarch
- 2 tablespoons butter
- 2 tablespoons olive oil
- 1/2 cup onion, minced
- 2 teaspoons fresh parsley, minced

Instructions:

1. In a bowl mix the broth, mustard, Worcestershire sauce, lemon juice, Sherry, Cognac, and cornstarch. Set aside.
2. In a heavy skillet or electric frying pan, heat the butter and oil over medium to medium-high heat, and sauté the steaks for about 3 to 5 minutes on each side. Remove the steaks to a platter and cover with foil.
3. In the skillet cook the minced onion over low-medium heat, until the onions are soft. Add the broth mixture and bring to a boil, stirring well (you might need to increase the heat somewhat).
4. The liquid should thicken considerably to the consistency of a gravy. Pour over the steaks and sprinkle some parsley over each steak.

Goes well with:

- Drinks: red wine, like a Barolo or a Merlot.
- Other recipes: salad with French Garlic dressing, vegetables.

Notes/Evaluation:

Veal Scaloppine with Marsala

Equipment needed:
meat pounder
wooden spoon

Special notes:
Marsala is an Italian (Sicilian) wine roughly comparable to a sherry. It does have a rather unique flavor, so if you substitute sherry you won't get the classical result. Marsala is also used for a wonderful dessert called zabaglione (see recipe).

Ingredients:
- 1 pound veal scaloppine
- 1/2 cup all purpose flour
- 1 teaspoon salt
- 1 teaspoon freshly ground pepper
- 2 tablespoons (or more) butter
- 2 tablespoons (or more) olive oil
- 1/2 cup Marsala wine
- 2 tablespoons chopped fresh parsley

Instructions:
1. Place the veal slices (one at a time) between sheets of wax paper and pound them (not too hard) till they're slightly less than 1/4-inch thick. You can use a meat pounder (use the flat side) or the bottom of a sturdy jar, or even a rolling pin.
2. Heat the butter and olive oil in a skillet over medium high heat.
3. Meanwhile, in a dish mix the flour with the salt and pepper. Lightly dredge the veal slices in flour mixture and shake off any excess.
4. Cook the veal a few pieces at a time until lightly browned on both sides. You might need to add a bit more butter and olive oil.
5. Remove the veal to a warmed serving plate and keep covered (with foil or a pan cover). (To warm the plate you can place it in the oven at the lowest setting.)
6. Into the drippings of the skillet stir in the Marsala. Bring to a boil, and with a wooden spoon scrape and mix any browned bits. Reduce the heat and simmer till the sauce has thickened. Pour the sauce over the meat, sprinkle with parsley, and serve.

Goes well with:
- Drinks: red wine, especially a lighter one like a Beaujolais.
- Other recipes: a salad, or a vegetable, or a side order of rice.

Notes/Evaluation:

Seafood

Cioppino (V)

Special notes:

This is a dish that comes from the Liguria region of Italy, where it is called "ciuppin." It is similar to bouillabaisse, the French version, but not as soupy. It is a very popular dish in San Francisco and, I imagine, most major cities that are a seaport. Basically, it is a combination of fish and shell fish (whatever is available) cooked with garlic, tomato, and various other ingredients.

Ingredients:

- 6 tablespoons olive oil
- 1 onion, minced
- 1 bell pepper, minced
- 1 celery stalk, minced
- 1 bunch green onions, cut into 1/2-inch pieces
- 2 garlic cloves, minced
- 1/4 cup chopped fresh parsley
- 1 can (28 ounces) Italian plum tomatoes (do NOT drain)
- 1/2 cup tomato sauce (1 medium size can)
- 1-1/2 cups red wine
- 2 bay leaves
- 1/2 teaspoon dried basil
- 1/2 teaspoon freshly ground pepper
- 1/2 teaspoon salt
- 12 mussels, well scrubbed
- 12 clams, well scrubbed
- 2 tablespoons olive oil
- 1 pound of fish cut into chunks (use a variety of fish, whatever is available, like red snapper, halibut, or trout)
- 1/2 pound sea scallops
- 1/2 pound shrimp, cleaned and deveined
- Dungeness crabs (sold live). Have them cleaned and cracked by your "fishperson" (or substitute 1/2 pound of cooked crab meat)

Instructions:

1. Heat the 6 tablespoons of olive oil in a large pot, over medium heat.
2. Add the onion, bell pepper, celery, green onions, garlic, and parsley, and cook for 10 to 12 minutes, stirring occasionally.
3. Add the tomatoes, tomato sauce, wine, bay leaves, basil, pepper, and salt. Bring to a boil, reduce the heat, cover the pot, and simmer for 90 minutes.
4. Meanwhile, clean the mussels and the clams by scrubbing under cold running water.
5. In a separate skillet, heat 2 tablespoons of olive oil, and add the mussels and clams. Cover the skillet and, using low to medium heat, heat the mussels and clams until they open. Discard any that do not.

6. Once they are opened, add the mussels and clams (with shells) to the large pot.
7. Stir in the fish, scallops, shrimp, and crab. Simmer for 20 to 30 minutes.
8. Serve like a soup from a tureen and ladle into individual bowls. Have one large bowl (or individual bowls) where the guests can place their empty shells. Eating cioppino is a bit of an art that requires both utensils and hands. If your guests are family or good friends, supply bibs or large napkins, and encourage them to use their hands.

Goes well with:

- Drinks: a red wine; try Montepulciano D'Abruzzo.
- Other recipes: French bread is a must; if you can get San Francisco type sourdough, then you've reached heaven!

Notes/Evaluation:

Fillet of Sole with Garlic Sauce (V)

Equipment needed:
skillet
pepper grinder

Special notes:
Other types of fish can be prepared this way.

Ingredients:
- 4 fillets of sole
- 3/4 cup of flour
- 1 teaspoon salt
- 1/2 teaspoon freshly ground pepper
- 3/4 cup olive oil
- 1/2 cup dry bread crumbs
- 4 garlic cloves, minced
- 2 tablespoons dry white wine (like Chablis)
- 2 tablespoons lemon juice

Instructions:
1. Make a mixture of the flour, salt, and pepper, and dredge each fillet in this mixture (easily done if the mixture is placed on a dish).
2. Heat a little bit of the olive oil (about 2 tablespoons) in a skillet over medium heat. When the oil is hot, cook the fillets until they are brown on both sides (turn gently with spatula).
3. While the fillets are frying, mix the bread crumbs with the garlic. Then add the rest of the olive oil, a little at a time, while mixing well with a fork, until the mixture has the consistency of mayonnaise.
4. Mix in the white wine and lemon juice. Remove the fillets from the skillet, and spread the bread crumb mixture over each piece. Serve.

Goes well with:
- Drinks: white wine, like Chablis or whatever was used in the recipe.
- Other recipes: a side dish of vegetables, like peas.

Notes/Evaluation:

Fish Fillets in Tomato Sauce (V)

Special notes:

When you buy the canned jalapenos, check for degree of hotness – you may wish to buy mild ones.

Ingredients:

- 1-1/2 pounds fish fillets (whatever is available)
- 2 tablespoons lemon juice (1 lemon)
- 2 tablespoons olive oil
- 1 garlic clove, minced
- 1 onion, sliced
- 1 green pepper, sliced into matchstick size pieces
- 4 small tomatoes, coarsely chopped
- 12 green olives, pitted
- 1 small can (4 ounces) diced jalapenos
- 1 small can (14-1/2 ounces) stewed tomatoes

Instructions:

1. Under cold running water, wash the fish fillets well. Drain and dry with paper towels. On a dish sprinkle each fillet with the lemon juice and set aside.
2. Heat the olive oil in a large skillet over medium heat.
3. Saute the garlic and onion in the skillet. Add green pepper and stir.
4. Add the fresh tomatoes, olives, jalapenos, and stewed tomatoes, and mix. Place the fish fillets in this sauce and cook uncovered 10 to 15 minutes, until the liquid thickens and the fish fillets are cooked (check with a fork – if they flake they are ready).
5. Place the fillets on a serving dish and spoon the sauce over them.

Goes well with:

- Drinks: white or red wine.
- Other recipes: vegetable medley or simple carrots.

Notes/Evaluation:

Grilled Salmon Steaks (V)

Special notes:

Few men need lessons on how to grill, since in American culture this has traditionally been a man's prerogative. Unfortunately, some men think of grilling as placing a slab of meat on a hot grill and letting the fire do the rest. Hopefully, this recipe might expand a few minds.

Ingredients:

For the marinade

- 3/4 cup dry white wine (like a Chardonnay)
- 1/2 cup vegetable oil
- 4 tablespoons lemon juice (2 lemons)
- 2 tablespoons minced parsley
- 2 teaspoons sugar
- 1 teaspoon Tabasco sauce
- 1/2 teaspoon salt
- 1/2 teaspoon dried oregano

- 4 salmon steaks
- cooking oil spray

Instructions:

1. Prepare the marinade. In a bowl mix well the wine, oil, lemon juice, parsley, sugar, Tabasco, oregano, and salt.
2. Place the salmon steaks in a large lockable plastic bag and pour the marinade over them. Seal the bag and place it in the refrigerator for at least 1 hour, occasionally "jostling" the marinade so the entire salmon steak is marinated.
3. Prepare your grill as usual. Make sure you spray oil on the racks so the steaks won't adhere to them.
4. Grill the steaks over medium heat for about 6 to 7 minutes on each side, until the salmon flakes when touched with a fork.

Goes well with:

- Drinks: a chilled white wine, like a Chardonnay.
- Other recipes: serve with a simple vegetable as a side dish.

Notes/Evaluation:

Marinated Grilled Shrimp

Equipment needed:

barbecue grill
wooden skewers

Special notes:

Some people like to clean and devein the shrimp, but I prefer to pay extra and let someone else do the surgery.

Ingredients:

For the marinade:

- 2 tablespoons chopped fresh parsley
- 4 tablespoons finely chopped fresh basil
- 4 garlic cloves, finely minced
- 1 teaspoon dried thyme
- 1 teaspoon freshly ground pepper
- 4 tablespoons fresh lemon juice (2 lemons)
- 6 tablespoons olive oil

- 24 large shrimp (cleaned and deveined) preferably fresh but probably "previously frozen"
- 4 to 6 wooden skewers (soak in water overnight)
- 4 green onions cut into 1-inch pieces
- 4 to 6 slices of bacon (cut into 2-inch pieces and doubled over)
- 24 bay leaves

Instructions:

1. In a large bowl mix well the first seven ingredients (from the parsley through the olive oil) to make the marinade.
2. Add the shrimp to the bowl and mix gently but well. Cover the bowl with plastic wrap and leave in the refrigerator to marinate overnight.
3. When ready, fire up your barbecue (spray your grill with cooking oil spray, so the food won't stick).
4. On each of the wooden skewers alternate shrimp, green onion, bacon, and bay leaf. Brush with the marinade
5. Place the skewers on the hot grill and grill for about 3 to 4 minutes on each side.
6. Serve on a platter.

Goes well with:

- Drinks: white wine, especially a Verdicchio (which typically comes in a fish shaped bottle.
- Other recipes: a salad; plain rice.

Notes/Evaluation:

SEAFOODD

Scallops with Lemon and Wine (V)

Equipment needed:
skillet

Special notes:
The taste of fish or seafood and lemon go particularly well together.

Ingredients:
- 1 pound scallops
- 2 tablespoons butter
- 1/3 cup dry white wine, like Sauterne or Rhine
- 1/3 cup vegetable broth, from a can or cube
- 5-10 drops Worcestershire sauce
- 1/2 teaspoon salt
- 2 lemons, 1 for juice and 1 cut into wedges
- freshly ground pepper
- parsley sprigs, for decoration

Instructions:
1. Rinse the scallops well under cold water, and dry using a paper towel.
2. Place the butter in a skillet, over medium heat.
3. When the butter has melted, cook the scallops for about 10 minutes, stirring frequently. Set aside, preferably on a warm serving platter.
4. In the skillet place the wine, broth, Worcestershire sauce, salt, and lemon juice. Turn the heat to high and cook to boiling. Stir well until the mixture is reduced to one-half.
5. Spoon the liquid mixture over the scallops, and garnish with ground pepper and, if you wish, parsley sprigs. If you like, serve with lemon wedges, to squeeze more juice on the scallops.

Goes well with:
- Drinks: white wine, the same you used in the recipe.
- Other recipes: a salad, a side serving of vegetables, crusty French bread.

Notes/Evaluation:

Shrimp with Aioli (V)

Equipment needed:
blender

Special notes:
Aioli is a garlic mayonnaise that is served with cold seafood and/or cold vegetables.

Ingredients:
- 4 large garlic cloves
- 2 tablespoons lemon juice (1 lemon)
- 3 egg yolks
- 1 cup olive oil
- 2 pounds cooked shrimp, cold
- 4 (or more) cups of mixed fresh vegetables (such as cauliflower, broccoli, mushrooms, green peppers, cherry tomatoes), cleaned and cut into pieces

Instructions:
1. To separate the yolks from the white part, simply crack the egg on the edge of a bowl. Let the white part run into the bowl, and save the yolks in a separate container.
2. In a blender place the garlic, lemon juice, and egg yolks, and blend until the mixture is smooth (about 1 minute or so).
3. With the blender running, add a cup of olive oil a few drops at a time, so the oil becomes incorporated into the paste. If at any point the oil is not being incorporated into the paste, stop the blender, add a couple of teaspoons of water, mix well, and continue blending.
4. You can serve the garlic mayonnaise immediately, or let it chill in the refrigerator for a couple of hours or more.
5. On one platter arrange the cold cooked shrimp, and on another the raw vegetables. Have the aioli in a small bowl, and guests can serve themselves by spooning some on their plate.

Goes well with:
- Drinks: white wine (if you feel brave, try Retsina, a Greek wine).
- Other recipes: depending on the amount of vegetables and people's appetites, this can be a meal in itself.

Notes/Evaluation:

Shrimp Tempura

Equipment needed:

wok (optional)
cooking thermometer (optional)

Special notes:

Tempura, a Japanese term, refers to food put into a batter and then fried. One can use various seafood (like crab legs) as well as some vegetables. This is a simple, basic version.

Ingredients:

- 2 cups ice cold water
- 2 cups all purpose flour
- 1-1/2 cups (or more) of vegetable oil
- 2 pounds medium or large shrimp, cleaned, deveined, and butterflied
- 1 jar Chinese mustard (optional)

For hot soy sauce (optional):

- 1 cup soy sauce
- 1/2 cup water
- 1/4 cup Sherry
- 1/2 cup brown sugar
- 2 teaspoons cornstarch

Instructions:

1. If your seafood provider did not butterfly the shrimp, you need to do so. This simply means to cut the shrimp lengthwise in half, but not all the way through so the open shrimp has a "butterfly" appearance. (Visualize a bagel; now visualize cutting it in half, but not the whole way, so the two halves are still attached, and when opened form the number 8; now you've got the technique of butterflying down pat!).

2. Prepare the batter. In a bowl place the ice water; gradually add 2 cups of flour as you stir. The batter should actually be lumpy rather than well mixed.

3. Heat the oil in a wok (or other pan). The oil should be about 3 inches in depth, enough to cover the shrimps as you fry them.

4. Once the oil is hot (if you have a cooking thermometer, it should register about 375 degrees), take each shrimp, dip it into the batter, and gently place it in the hot oil (use metal tongs and be careful of any spatterings).

5. Let the shrimp cook for about 1 or 2 minutes on each side. Cook as many shrimp as will fit in the wok, but don't crowd them. As they are done, drain on paper towels and keep warm (you might have an ovenproof container in the oven, set at about 125 degrees, where you can place the fried shrimp).

6. Serve with Chinese mustard and/or hot soy sauce in serving bowls. To prepare the hot soy sauce, mix the indicated ingredients in a small pan, and bring it to a boil.

Goes well with:

- Drinks: Japanese beer.
- Other recipes: raw chewy vegetables like carrots and celery; a salad.

Notes/Evaluation:

Trout baked in parchment paper

Special notes:

You can use trout or some other type of fish like mackerel, red snapper, or sea bass. Parchment paper is available in many supermarkets.

Ingredients:

- 4 medium-sized trouts (12 to 16 ounces each. Have the butcher clean them. The head and tail can stay or be removed).
- Parchment paper
- 8 tablespoons olive oil
- 2 teaspoons salt
- 2 teaspoons freshly ground pepper
- 8 bay leaves
- 4 slices of lemon, cut in half
- 4 slices bacon
- 4 teaspoons finely minced garlic (about 4 cloves)
- 4 tablespoons minced parsley
- 4 tablespoons chopped onion
- 4 teaspoons dried oregano
- 8 tablespoons dry white wine (like Chardonnay)

Instructions:

1. Preheat the oven to 400 degrees.
2. Wash the fish well under cold running water. Dry well with paper towels.
3. Cut 4 pieces of parchment paper, each about 16 inches long or long enough to wrap around the fish loosely.
4. Lay the paper flat on a work surface. Brush 1 tablespoon of olive oil on the inside of each piece of parchment paper. If you have the space, do all four pieces; otherwise do one at a time.
5. Place a fish in the center of the paper. Sprinkle the salt and the pepper (1/2 teaspoon for each fish) both outside and inside the fish. Place 2 bay leaves and a slice (two halves) of lemon in the cavity of each fish. Wrap a piece of bacon around each fish.
6. Drizzle a tablespoon of olive oil on each fish, a teaspoon of chopped garlic, a tablespoon of minced parsley, a tablespoon of chopped onion, a teaspoon of oregano, and two tablespoons of white wine.
7. Fold the parchment paper loosely around the trout, but tightly sealed at the ends.

8. Bake in an oven-proof dish for 25 to 30 minutes.
9. To serve, place each parchment envelope on an individual dish. Be careful when opening the parchment as steam may be present.

Goes well with:

- Drinks: white wine (either what's left from the ingredients or something else like a Pinot Grigio).
- Other recipes: crusty bread; side order of oven roasted potatoes; a salad; polenta as a first course.

Notes/Evaluation:

Steamed Mussels and Clams with Chorizo

Equipment needed:
slotted spoon (optional)
sieve

Special notes:
Chorizo is a Mexican sausage and can be quite spicy. If not available, you can use Italian sausage (hot or mild) or Polish sausage (Kielbasa).

Ingredients:
- 2 pounds fresh mussels (in shell)
- 2 pounds fresh clams (in shell)
- 6 tablespoons olive oil
- 4 cloves of garlic, finely minced
- 1 cup dry white wine (like Chardonnay)
- 1/2 cup water, boiling
- 8 chorizo links (or other sausage)
- 2 tablespoons lemon juice (1 lemon)
- 4 tablespoons chopped fresh parsley
- 1 teaspoon freshly ground pepper

Instructions:
1. Scrub and rinse the mussels and clams under cold water. If the mussels have a "beard," cut it off and scrub well.
2. Heat the olive oil in a large pot over medium heat. Add the garlic and sauté (don't let the garlic burn – if necessary lower the heat). Add the wine.
3. Add the mussels and clams, increase the heat to medium high, and cover the pot.
4. Heat for about 10 minutes, occasionally shaking the pot.
5. Meanwhile, heat 1/2 cup of water to boiling.
6. Using a slotted spoon, remove the mussels and clams to a separate bowl. Discard any that have not opened. Cover the bowl with foil to keep warm.
7. Add the boiling water and sausage links to the pot. Cover the pot, lower the heat to medium, and simmer for about 15 minutes (if you are using precooked sausage like Kielbasa, simmer for only 5 minutes).
8. Take the mussels and clams and place them back in the pot. Cook everything about 5 to 10 more minutes.
9. To serve, place the mussels, clams, and sausage on a serving bowl or platter, preferably in an attractive pattern. Then using a sieve, strain the liquid over them. Sprinkle with lemon juice, parsley, and pepper.

Goes well with:
- Drinks: white wine; beer.
- Other recipes: crusty French bread, especially to soak up the juice; a small salad as a side dish.

Pasta

Fettucine Alfredo (V)

Equipment needed:
colander
large bowl
pepper grinder

Special notes:
Another classic recipe that is easy to prepare. There are many variations of this dish; some omit the half-and-half, some use more butter, some add peas or garlic or other ingredients.

Ingredients:
- 1 pound fettucine
- 1 cup half-and-half
- 4 tablespoons sweet (unsalted) butter, softened
- 1/2 cup freshly grated Parmesan cheese (preferably from a cheese shop)
- freshly ground black pepper

Instructions:
1. Cook the fettucine in a pot (6- or 8-quart) of boiling salted water. Follow the manufacturer's directions. Do not overcook – cook "al dente," firm and not mushy.
2. While the water is boiling, in a large bowl (preferably warmed), mix the half-and-half and the butter (cut the butter into small pieces or mash gently with a fork).
3. When the fettucine are ready, drain in the colander and place in the bowl with the cream sauce. Add the cheese and mix well.
4. Serve with a little ground pepper on top, and extra cheese if needed.

Goes well with:
- Drinks: red or dry white wine.
- Other recipes: salad, French bread.

Notes/Evaluation:

Fettucine with Lemon Sauce (V)

Equipment needed:

colander

Special notes:

This is a popular Italian recipe, easy to prepare.

Ingredients:

- 1 pound fettucine (spaghetti, or other long shape)
- 2 teaspoons salt
- 1 cup heavy cream (also called whipping cream) (= 1/2 pint)
- 4 tablespoons butter
- 4 lemons, grate the rind and squeeze the juice (grate before you cut the lemons)
- 2 tablespoons lemon juice (from 1 lemon)
- grated Parmesan cheese, preferably from a cheese shop

Instructions:

1. Fill a large (6- or 8-quart) pot 3/4 with water and heat. When the water is boiling, add 2 teaspoons of salt, and cook the fettucine according to the package directions.
2. While the water is heating, place the cream and butter in a pan over medium high to high heat. If you use a somewhat small pan, be careful the cream and butter do not overflow or burn. If they start to, simply lift the pan from the heat. When they begin to boil, add grated lemon rind and lemon juice and stir constantly, till the volume is reduced to about one half.
3. When the pasta is ready, drain it and then put it back in the pot. Add the lemon sauce and mix thoroughly.
4. Serve with grated cheese.

Goes well with:

- Drinks: red wine, especially a Chianti or a Soave.
- Other recipes: salad, French bread.

Notes/Evaluation:

Linguine al Pesto (V)

Equipment needed:

food processor or blender
colander

Special notes:

You can buy pesto sauce already made, but there's nothing like homemade pesto. You can serve pesto on pasta, on crackers as an appetizer, as a topping to a pizza, as topping to a tomato salad, or mixed with virgin olive oil as a dipping for focaccia (bread). For a variation, you can use walnuts instead of pine nuts.

Ingredients:

- 2 cups fresh basil leaves
- 1 cup freshly grated Parmesan cheese
- 1/3 cup pine nuts
- 2 cloves garlic
- 1/4 teaspoon salt
- 1/4 teaspoon freshly ground pepper
- 1/2 cup virgin olive oil

- 1 pound linguine (or spaghetti)
- 1 cup additional grated Parmesan cheese for serving

Instructions:

1. Place the first six ingredients (basil through pepper) in a food processor (or blender) and blend well. Slowly add the olive oil to make a thick paste.

2. If you make the sauce separately for future use or don't intend to use all of it, place in a small jar, top with a bit of olive oil, and keep in refrigerator. If you use only part of it, always top with olive oil, or the basil will darken (still edible but not aesthetically pleasing).

3. Fill a 6-quart (or larger) pot 2/3 full of water and bring to a boil over high heat. Add a tablespoon of salt.

4. Place the linguine in the boiling water and follow the cooking directions on the package. If a cooking time is not given (and often it is not) try cooking for 10 to 11 minutes, and then taste one of the strands (whatever you do, DON't throw the strand against the wall to see if it sticks, and DON't add olive oil, cold water, or anything else to the boiling water). Continue cooking until the pasta is "al dente," that is, solid to the bite and not under- or overcooked.

5. Before you drain the pasta, save a cup of the boiling water (simply dip in the pot with a measuring cup or a ladle). Drain the pasta in a colander.

6. In a serving bowl place 3 to 5 tablespoons of the pesto. If it is too thick dilute it with some of the pasta water. Add the pasta and mix it well. If necessary add more pesto and more water (but use the water sparingly – the pesto should be thick rather than runny).

7. Serve with grated parmesan cheese. Some people prefer no extra cheese, since they want to savor the pesto flavor (and the pesto already contains cheese).

Goes well with:
- Drinks: red or white wine; I prefer a light red.
- Other recipes: crusty bread; can be a meal in itself.

Notes/Evaluation:

Linguine alla Giorgio (V)

Equipment needed:

baking sheet
colander
pepper grinder

Special notes:

To simplify the recipe, you don't need to char the bell pepper.

Ingredients:

- 1 pound linguine
- 1 teaspoon salt
- 1 red or yellow bell pepper (if you must, use a green one)
- 1-1/2 tablespoons of olive oil
- 2 garlic cloves, minced
- 1/2 cup canned Italian tomatoes (chopped)
- 1 tablespoon capers
- 2 anchovies, diced (use canned ones)
- 12 pitted black olives, minced
- juice of 1 lemon
- 1/4 teaspoon oregano (dry or fresh)
- 1/4 teaspoon rosemary (dry or fresh)
- freshly ground black pepper
- freshly grated Parmesan cheese

Instructions:

1. Fill a large (6- or 8-quart) pot two-thirds with water and heat to boiling. When the water boils, add 1 teaspoon of salt. When the water boils again, add the linguine and cook according to the manufacturer's directions.

2. While the water is heating, prepare the sauce. First place the bell pepper on a cookie sheet and broil in the oven, about 5 inches away from the heat source. Turn frequently. When the bell pepper is charred on the outside, remove from oven, let cool and peel (or rub the peel with a towel to remove it). Cut the pepper into 1/2-inch pieces.

3. In a skillet heat the olive oil over medium heat.

4. Add the garlic and sauté, stirring frequently, for about 2 to 3 minutes.

5. Add the tomatoes and their juice, and cook for 5 to 7 minutes, stirring frequently.

6. Add the bell pepper, capers, anchovies, olives, lemon juice, oregano, and rosemary. Mix well and let simmer 3 to 5 minutes, until everything is heated.

7. Drain the pasta when it is cooked (see package instructions or use 9 to 11 minutes as a guide). Place in a serving bowl, and pour the sauce over the linguine. Mix well and serve. For those who want, grind some black pepper over the dish. Have grated Parmesan cheese available at the table.

Goes well with:

- Drinks: red wine (a Chianti or even a Pinot Noir).
- Other recipes: a salad.

Notes/Evaluation:

Linguine, Torino Style (V)

Equipment needed:

heavy skillet
large (6- or 8-quart) pot

Special notes:

Pine nuts can be found in specialty stores; usually a bit expensive.

Ingredients:

- 1 pound linguine (or spaghetti, or other pasta)

- 1/4 cup pine nuts
- 4 tablespoons breadcrumbs, seasoned Italian

- 1/2 cup olive oil
- 4 garlic cloves, minced
- 1/4 teaspoon cayenne pepper
- 1/4 cup parsley, minced
- salt and freshly ground pepper
- grated Parmesan cheese, preferably from cheese shop

Instructions:

1. Fill large pot 2/3 with water and place on stove over high heat. When the water boils, cook linguine following the manufacturer's instructions.

2. While the water is heating, place the pine nuts in a small pan over medium to high medium heat and roast (don't let them burn). After about 3 to 5 minutes, add the bread crumbs and toast both till they are golden. Set aside.

3. In a heavy skillet set over medium low heat, heat the olive oil. Add the garlic and cayenne pepper; stir and cook until garlic is golden brown. With a slotted spoon, remove the garlic and discard.

4. When the linguine are cooked, drain (but not too well), and return the linguine to the pot. Add the oil and mix well. Add the pine nut and breadcrumb mixture, the parsley, the freshly ground pepper (I like a fair amount), and a little bit of salt, and mix well.

5. Serve with grated cheese.

Goes well with:

- Drinks: a robust red wine, like Bardolino or Burgundy.

- Other recipes: salad, French bread, vegetables.

Notes/Evaluation:

Linguine with White Clam Sauce (V)

Equipment needed:
- large (6- to 8-quartt) pot
- skillet
- colander
- pepper grinder

Special notes:
One of my favorites – every restaurant seems to offer this, but each is unique. This is the kind of recipe that is easy to experiment with. For example, increase (or decrease) the amount of butter. Use more (or less) garlic. Use more (or less) lemon juice. Add a bit of grated lemon rind.

Ingredients:
- 1 pound linguine (or spaghetti)

- 4 tablespoons butter
- 4 tablespoons olive oil
- 3 garlic cloves, minced
- 1 can minced clams
- 1/4 cup white wine (like Chablis, Chardonnay, or Pinot Grigio)
- 1 lemon, juice only
- freshly ground black pepper
- grated parmesan cheese

Instructions:
1. In a pot of boiling salted water cook the linguine according to the manufacturer's instructions. Cook "al dente" – firm to the bite, not mushy.
2. While the water is boiling, heat the butter and the oil in a skillet over low to medium heat. Saute the garlic for 1 or 2 minutes, add the clams with their juice, add the white wine, and simmer uncovered for about 10 minutes.
3. When the linguine are cooked, drain, place in a serving bowl and mix well with the clams and the lemon juice. Sprinkle with pepper. Serve with grated cheese, available at the table.

Goes well with:
- Drinks: white or red wine.
- Other recipes: salad; crusty bread; chicken.

Notes/Evaluation:

Linguine with Garlic & Hazelnut Sauce (V)

Equipment needed:

baking sheet
pepper grinder

Special notes:

Hazelnuts are a favorite of Northern Italians and used quite frequently in their cuisine. This is a simple recipe that illustrates the fact that almost anything can be used as a topping for pasta.

Ingredients:

- 4 garlic cloves – unpeeled
- 2 tablespoons shelled hazelnuts
- 2 tablespoons olive oil
- 1/4 teaspoon salt
- 1/4 teaspoon freshly ground pepper
- 1 pound linguine (or spaghetti)
- grated Parmesan cheese (preferably fresh from the deli)

Instructions:

1. Preheat the broiler in your oven.
2. On a baking sheet lined with heavy-duty foil, broil the garlic cloves 4 to 5 inches away from the heat source; turn the garlic frequently until charred on all sides. Remove from the oven and let cool.
3. Turn the oven to 300 degrees. Place the hazelnuts on a baking sheet and roast until they are browned (about 10 minutes). Shake the sheet frequently as they roast. Place the hazelnuts on a clean kitchen towel and rub in the towel to remove the brown skins of the nuts. Chop the hazelnuts fine.
4. Fill a large pot (6 or 8 quarts) two-thirds with water and bring to a boil. Add 2 teaspoons salt, and when the water is boiling again, add the pasta. Cook the linguine according to the manufacturer's directions.
5. While the linguine are cooking, discard the skins of the garlic cloves and place in a small bowl. Add the olive oil and mash into a paste, using the back of a fork.
6. Place the garlic mixture in a small skillet, and heat over medium heat for 2 to 4 minutes, stirring constantly. Add salt and pepper, stir, and remove from heat.

7. When the linguine are cooked "al dente," drain, place in a serving platter or bowl, and toss with the garlic mixture, the minced hazelnuts, and some of the Parmesan cheese. Serve additional cheese at the table.

Goes well with:

- Drinks: red wine.
- Other recipes: pasta can be a meal in itself, or can be served with a small salad, or side dish of vegetables.

Notes/Evaluation:

Linguine with Zucchini & Green Onions (V)

Equipment needed:

colander
pepper grinder

Special notes:

Don't overcook the vegetables – they are best when crisp.

Ingredients:

- 1 pound linguine (or spaghetti)
- 3 tablespoons butter
- 3 tablespoons olive oil
- 2 small zucchinis, cleaned, trimmed, and minced
- 2 green onions, cleaned, trimmed, and minced
- 2 garlic cloves, minced
- freshly ground pepper
- salt
- 2 tablespoons parsley, minced
- Parmesan grated cheese

Instructions:

1. Clean the zucchinis and the green onions by washing under cold water. You might need to scrub the zucchinis with a vegetable brush. Cut and discard the ends of the zucchinis. Cut and discard most of the green portion of the green onion. Mince both the zucchinis and the green onions.

2. In a pot of boiling salted water (about 1 tablespoon or less of salt), cook the linguine according to the manufacturer's instructions. Cook "al dente," firm to the bite, not mushy.

3. While the water is heating, heat the butter and olive oil in a large skillet over low to medium heat. Add the zucchinis and green onions, and sauté for about 3 to 5 minutes, so the vegetables are crisp.

4. Add the garlic and sauté for 1-2 minutes more, till the garlic is golden brown.

5. When the pasta is cooked, drain and place in serving bowl. Add the butter-oil mixture and mix well. Add pepper and salt to taste, and sprinkle the parsley on top.

6. Serve at the table with grated cheese.

Goes well with:

- Drinks: red wine.
- Other recipes: salad; crusty bread; chicken.

Notes/Evaluation:

Penne with Tomato sauce (V)

Equipment needed:

pepper grinder (optional)
colander for pasta

Special notes:

Pasta comes in hundreds of shapes, such as bow ties (farfalle), little tubes (rigatoni), shells (conchiglie), linguine, and so on. This recipe calls for penne, which are little tubes whose ends are cut at an angle. You could however, substitute rigatoni, farfalle, or any other shape you wish.

Ingredients:

- 2 tablespoons olive oil
- 3 garlic cloves, minced
- 1 yellow onion, finely diced
- 1/2 cup diced celery
- 3 pounds Roma (plum) tomatoes, finely diced
- 2 tablespoons chopped parsley
- 1 teaspoon dried thyme
- 1 teaspoon dried basil
- 2 tablespoons lemon juice (1 lemon)
- 1 teaspoon sugar
- 1/2 teaspoon salt
- 1/2 teaspoon freshly ground pepper
- 1 cup red wine

- 1 pound penne (or other pasta)
- 1/2 cup or more freshly grated Parmesan cheese

Instructions:

1. In a 6-quart pan heat the olive oil over medium heat. Add the garlic and sauté for about a minute. Add the onion and the celery and sauté for about 3 to 5 minutes.
2. Stir in the tomatoes and cook for about 10 to 12 minutes until the sauce begins to thicken.
3. Add all the other ingredients (up to and including the wine), stir well, and simmer for about 10 to 15 minutes.
4. While the sauce simmers, prepare the penne according to the package instructions.
5. When "al dente," serve the penne with the sauce, and have available Parmesan cheese.

Goes well with:

- Drinks: red or white wine.
- Other recipes: crusty bread; a salad; Tuscan bean dip for the bread.

Notes/Evaluation:

Spaghetti alla Bolognese

Equipment needed:

pepper grinder
colander for pasta

Special notes:

Bolognese sauce, named after the city of Bologna, is another classic pasta sauce, one that emphasizes the meat flavor rather than the tomato flavor. Pancetta is an Italian "ham" that is very flavorful. If you can't find it (but do try), use bacon.

Ingredients:

- 2 tablespoons olive oil
- 1/4 cup diced pancetta (or bacon)
- 1/2 onion minced
- 1 carrot, peeled and minced
- 1 celery stalk, minced
- 1/2 pound ground chuck
- 1/2 pound ground pork
- 1/2 cup dry white wine
- 1 can (28 ounces) pureed tomatoes
- 2 tablespoons tomato paste (comes in small can)
- 1/4 cup of milk
- 2 teaspoons sugar
- 1 teaspoon salt
- 1 teaspoon freshly ground pepper
- 1 teaspoon dried oregano
- 1 pound spaghetti
- grated Parmesan cheese

Instructions:

1. Heat the oil in a large pan, over medium heat.
2. Add the diced pancetta (or bacon) and cook for about 5 minutes.
3. Add the onion, carrot, and celery, and cook for another 5 minutes.
4. Add the meat (the chuck and the pork) and stir, letting it brown.
5. When all the meat is browned, stir in the wine, pureed tomatoes, and tomato paste. Lower the heat to low and let the sauce simmer for one hour, stirring occasionally.
6. Stir in the milk, sugar, salt, pepper, and oregano, and let simmer for another 45 minutes.
7. About 30 minutes before the sauce is ready (i.e., 15 minutes after step #6), prepare the water for the spaghetti and cook according to the directions on the package (see section on cooking pasta).
8. Add the sauce to the spaghetti in a bowl and toss. You should have extra spaghetti sauce to serve at the table. Have grated Parmesan cheese (preferably from a cheese shop or deli).

Goes well with:

- Drinks: red wine; I prefer a lighter one that doesn't overwhelm the sauce – like a Valpolicella or Bardolino.
- Other recipes: serve with crusty bread and a small salad.

Spaghetti alla Carbonara

Equipment needed:

large skillet
colander
pepper grinder

Special notes:

The word "carbone" means charcoal in Italian, and this sauce is in the "charcoal-seller's style." Other pasta shapes can also be used, such as rigatoni, penne, bow ties, etc. If you cannot find the Pecorino cheese (a type of Parmesan cheese, very sharp), simply double the amount of Parmesan cheese.

Ingredients:

- 1 to 2 tablespoons of butter
- 4 teaspoons olive oil
- 1 clove garlic, crushed (use both juice and pulp)
- 6 slices of bacon, diced
- 1 pound of spaghetti (or other pasta)
- 5 eggs
- pinch of salt
- 5 tablespoons grated Parmesan cheese
- 5 tablespoons grated Pecorino cheese
- 1 tablespoon or more freshly ground black pepper

Instructions:

1. In a large skillet, over medium heat, heat the butter and the olive oil. When they are hot, sauté the garlic and the bacon. Discard the garlic as soon as it is lightly brown.

2. In a large pan of boiling salted water, cook the spaghetti following the manufacturer's directions. As always, cook "al dente" – do not overcook.

3. Meanwhile, beat the eggs thoroughly in a large serving bowl, with a pinch of salt, the two cheeses, and the freshly ground black pepper. You can use an electric or hand egg beater, or a fork.

4. As soon as the spaghetti is cooked, drain, and place back in the pan. Add the egg and cheese mixture and the butter-oil-bacon to the pan. Over low heat cook and stir for a couple of minutes, so the egg mixture is heated.

5. Serve on a serving platter or pasta bowl.

Goes well with:

- Drinks: red wine.
- Other recipes: a small salad.

Notes/Evaluation:

Spaghetti alla Puttanesca (Spaghetti Prostitute Style) (V)

Equipment needed:

colander
pepper grinder

Special notes:

In Italian puttanesca means "prostitute style"; the name of this dish supposedly reflects the ease with which this sauce can be prepared – even by a prostitute between clients!

Ingredients:

- 1/3 cup olive oil
- 3 garlic cloves, minced
- 1 can (28 ounces) peeled tomatoes (or 6 medium to large fresh tomatoes, chopped)
- 12-16 large black olives, pitted (preferably from deli)
- 1 tablespoon capers
- 1/2 teaspoon dried oregano
- 1 teaspoon dried red pepper
- 1/2 teaspoon freshly ground black pepper
- 1 can anchovy fillets
- 2-3 sprigs parsley, minced
- salt

- 1 pound spaghetti
- grated parmesan cheese

Instructions:

1. In a large skillet, over medium heat, heat the oil and sauté the garlic until lightly browned.
2. Add the tomatoes, olives, capers, oregano, red and black pepper, and cook over medium heat for 15 to 20 minutes, till the sauce thickens. Be careful as the oil may spatter when you add the tomatoes.
3. Cut the anchovies into small pieces and stir into the sauce, together with the parsley. Cook gently for about 2 minutes. If you like, add a little salt to taste, and let the sauce simmer over low heat, for about 20 to 30 minutes.
4. While the sauce simmers, cook the spaghetti in a pan of boiling salted water, following the manufacturer's recommendations.
5. When the spaghetti is cooked "al dente" (firm, not mushy), drain, place in a serving bowl, and mix well with the sauce.
6. Serve with freshly grated Parmesan cheese.

Goes well with:

- Drinks: a hearty red wine, like Burgundy.
- Other recipes: a salad, French bread.

Notes/Evaluation:

Spaghetti alla Toscana (V)

Equipment needed:

heavy non-aluminum pan
colander

Special notes:

Another basic Italian spaghetti sauce. This one can be made ahead and refrigerated for later use.

Ingredients:

- 1/4 cup olive oil
- 1/2 cup minced carrots
- 1 cup minced onion
- 1/2 cup minced parsley
- 1/2 cup minced celery
- 1 teaspoon dried basil
- 3 garlic cloves minced
- 2 cans peeled tomatoes, Italian style (usually 28 ounces per can)
- 1 pound spaghetti
- 1 teaspoon salt
- freshly grated parmesan cheese

Instructions:

1. In a heavy 4- or 6-quart non-aluminum pan, heat the oil over medium heat.
2. When the oil is hot, add the carrots, onions, parsley, and celery, and brown, stirring frequently, for about 10 minutes.
3. Add the basil, garlic, and tomatoes, and mix well.
4. Reduce the heat to low and simmer for about 30 to 45 minutes, until the sauce is thick.
5. While the sauce is simmering, fill a large pot (6 quarts) two-thirds with water and heat to boiling. When the water is boiling, add 1 teaspoon of salt. When the water comes to a boil again, add the spaghetti and cook following the manufacturer's instructions. Cook the spaghetti "al dente," firm to the bite, not mushy.
6. Drain the pasta when it is cooked. Place in a serving bowl and pour some of the sauce over it. Serve with freshly grated Parmesan cheese.

Goes well with:

- Drinks: a hearty red wine like Chianti or Burgundy.
- Other recipes: a salad or a side dish of vegetables.

Notes/Evaluation:

Spaghetti al Tonno (V)

Equipment needed:

large pot (6- or 8-quart size)
colander
pepper grinder

Special notes:

Despite its simplicity, this is a delicious and rapidly prepared dish.

Ingredients:

- 1 lb. Spaghetti (or other pasta like linguine)
- 1 can of tuna
- 6-8 leaves of fresh basil, minced
- 2 tomatoes, chopped
- 1/4 cup olive oil
- 1 tablespoon lemon juice
- 1/2 teaspoon salt
- 1/2 teaspoon freshly ground pepper

Instructions:

1. Place a pot of water on the stove to cook the spaghetti. Follow the package directions but make sure the spaghetti is cooked "al dente," not overcooked and mushy. If there are no directions, cook for 10 minutes, taste a strand, and continue cooking if necessary, checking at 1- or 2-minute intervals.
2. While the pasta is cooking (or before), place all other ingredients in a bowl and mix gently. If the tuna is in water, drain the water.
3. When the spaghetti is cooked, drain and place in serving bowl – add the tuna mixture and enjoy. If you wish, top with Parmesan cheese.

Goes well with:

- Drinks: dry white wine or red; I like Verdicchio or a Gamay.
- Other recipes: a salad; a nice dessert like baked pears.

Notes/Evaluation:

Spaghetti Sauce a la Marinara (V)

Equipment needed:

saucepans
colander

Special notes:

A basic sauce for spaghetti. There are many versions of this. If you like, you can add anchovy fillets, minced parsley (3 tablespoons). You can also cut down on the tomato paste and/or eliminate the red wine.

Ingredients:

- 1 lb. Spaghetti (or other pasta like linguine)
- 4 tablespoons olive oil
- 2 garlic cloves, minced
- 2 onions, chopped finely
- 1 teaspoon dried oregano
- 2 dried sage leaves (or 1/2 teaspoon flaked)
- 3 teaspoons dried basil
- 1 tablespoon sugar
- 2 teaspoon salt
- 8-10 fresh tomatoes, chopped finely
- 2 cans tomato paste (6 oz. each)
- 1/4 cup red wine (like Burgundy, Chianti, etc.)
- grated Parmesan cheese

Instructions:

1. In a saucepan (2 quarts or larger) heat the olive oil over low to medium heat. When hot, cook the garlic and onions until they are tender.
2. Add all other ingredients and mix well.
3. Increase heat to high until mixture boils. Then reduce heat to simmer for 30 minutes, mixing occasionally.
4. Place a pot of water on the stove to cook the spaghetti. Follow the package directions (usually 10 to 12 minutes), but make sure the spaghetti is cooked "al dente" – not mushy or overcooked.
5. Drain the spaghetti, place in a serving bowl, add the sauce, mix well, and serve with grated cheese.

Goes well with:

- Drinks: red wine, such as Burgundy, Chianti, Pinot Noir, etc.
- Other recipes: garlic bread; a salad; serve pears and cheese for dessert.

Notes/Evaluation:

Spaghetti Sauce a la Portofino (V)

Equipment needed:

frying pan
saucepan
pepper grinder
colander

Special notes:

Don't let the 10 garlic cloves scare you!

Ingredients:

- 1 lb. Spaghetti (or other pasta)
- 6 medium to large tomatoes
- 1 cup diced onion
- 1/2 cup diced celery
- 10 garlic cloves, minced
- 2 tablespoons fresh basil, minced
- 1/4 teaspoon salt
- 1/4 teaspoon freshly ground pepper
- 4 tablespoons olive oil

Instructions:

1. Heat the oil in a frying pan over medium-low heat.
2. Saute the onion and the celery, until the onion is browned and the celery is softened (about 10 minutes).
3. Add the garlic, basil, salt and pepper. Stir and let cool.
4. Drop the tomatoes in a pan of boiling water for 30 to 45 seconds to loosen their skins. Remove tomatoes, rinse under cool water, and peel.
5. Chop the tomatoes finely and stir into the sautéed ingredients.
6. Cook the spaghetti according to the package directions. Drain and place in serving bowl. Add the sauce.

Goes well with:

- Drinks: red wine.
- Other recipes: garlic toast; a salad.

Notes/Evaluation:

Spaghetti Sauce with Mushrooms (V)

Equipment needed:

saucepan

Special notes:

A basic sauce for pasta. Once you have mastered this recipe, you should try to experiment by, for example, varying the proportion of ingredients (less salt, fewer or more mushrooms, etc.), or adding new ingredients (perhaps you have some oregano, or a carrot, or...).

Ingredients:

- 1 cup chopped onion
- 2 garlic cloves, minced
- 1/4 cup olive oil (or vegetable oil)
- 1/2 pound mushrooms, sliced (or 2 cans)
- 1 teaspoon salt
- 1/4 teaspoon thyme
- 2 large cans of peeled tomatoes
- 1 lb. Spaghetti (or other pasta)
- freshly grated Parmesan cheese

Instructions:

1. In a saucepan heat the olive oil over medium heat.
2. Lightly sauté the onion and the garlic for about 10 minutes, until the onion is wilted.
3. Add the mushrooms and sauté for about 10 minutes. Season with salt and thyme and stir gently.
4. Add tomatoes and simmer the sauce for about 60 to 90 minutes. Keep the heat low so the sauce doesn't burn or dry out. Keep the lid on the pan so the water doesn't evaporate. If the sauce seems a bit thick, add a little bit of water, or tomato juice, or white wine. This sauce can be made ahead, and simply reheated when you need it, although it is best when freshly made. Store in refrigerator.
5. Otherwise cook 1 pound of spaghetti (or other pasta) according to package directions. Drain, place in serving bowl, and toss with sauce. Serve with grated Parmesan cheese.

Goes well with:

- Drinks: red wine, like a Burgundy or a Merlot.
- Other recipes: French bread; a salad.

Notes/Evaluation:

Spaghetti "Aglio e Olio" (Spaghetti with Garlic & Oil) (V)

Equipment needed:
colander
pepper grinder

Special notes:
A very easy recipe; if you are an anchovy "aficionado," add some to this recipe as you sauté the garlic (and omit the salt).

Ingredients:
- 1 pound spaghetti (or linguine)
- 1/3 cup olive oil
- 4 garlic cloves, minced
- freshly ground pepper
- salt
- 2 tablespoons parsley, minced
- grated Parmesan cheese

Instructions:
1. In a pot of boiling salted water cook the pasta according to the package directions. Cook "al dente" – firm to the bite, not mushy.
2. While the water is boiling, heat the oil in a skillet, over low to medium heat. Add the garlic and sauté until the garlic is light brown. Do not burn and stir frequently.
3. When the pasta is cooked, drain and place in a serving bowl. Mix well with the oil and garlic, add some pepper and salt, and top with the parsley.
4. Have grated Parmesan cheese available at the table.

Goes well with:
- Drinks: red or white wine.
- Other recipes: salad; crusty bread; chicken.

Notes/Evaluation:

Spaghetti with Anchovies, Capers & Olives (V)

Equipment needed:

colander
pepper grinder

Special notes:

Quite simple to prepare, but very flavorful.

Ingredients:

- 1 pound spaghetti (or linguine, etc.)
- 1/2 cup olive oil
- 2 garlic cloves, cut in quarters
- 1 can pitted black olives, cut in quarters
- 1 small jar (4 ounces) capers
- 1/4 cup parsley, minced
- 4 tablespoons water
- 2 teaspoons freshly ground black pepper
- 1 can (2 ounces) flat anchovy fillets, minced
- grated Parmesan cheese

Instructions:

1. Fill a large pot two-thirds with water and heat to boiling. When the water is boiling, cook the spaghetti according to package directions.
2. While the water is boiling, prepare the sauce. In a skillet heat the oil. Add the garlic and sauté till the garlic is golden brown. Remove the garlic and discard.
3. Add the olives, capers, parsley, water, and black pepper, and cook for 5 minutes.
4. Remove from the heat. Add the anchovies and stir till the anchovies dissolve.
5. Drain the pasta when it is cooked. Place in a serving bowl, pour the sauce over the pasta and mix well. Have grated cheese available at the table.

Goes well with:

- Drinks: a hearty red wine like a Pinot Noir, a Burgundy, or a Chianti.
- Other recipes: French bread; a salad.

Notes/Evaluation:

Spaghetti with Mushrooms & Sausage

Equipment needed:

egg slicer for the mushrooms
pepper grinder (optional)
colander

Special notes:

Pasta can be topped with an incredible variety of ingredients (please don't try pineapple…). Two that go very well are mushrooms and sausage.

Ingredients:

- 8 to 12 ounces of Italian sausage (about 4 to 6 links)
- 1/2 cup chopped onion
- 2 cups sliced mushrooms
- 2 garlic cloves, minced
- 1/2 teaspoon dried oregano
- 1/2 teaspoon salt
- 1/2 teaspoon freshly ground pepper
- 2 cans tomato sauce (8 ounces each)
- 1 pound spaghetti (or fettucine or even rigatoni)
- freshly grated Parmesan cheese

Instructions:

1. Clean the mushrooms by wiping each with a damp paper towel, and with a knife remove the end of each stem (about the thickness of a dime). Slice each mushroom (use an egg slicer and you'll get perfect, even slices).

2. Fill a 6-quart (or larger) pan 2/3 with water and heat to boiling over high heat.

3. While the water is heating, remove the sausage meat from the casings by squeezing in the middle of each link, and pulling apart (or you can buy the sausage meat that's not in the casings). In a large skillet cook the sausage over medium heat; with a fork break up and mix the meat, until it is all lightly browned. Transfer the meat to a dish. If there is a lot of oil (fat) in the skillet, remove it (pour it into an empty can), and leave only about 2 tablespoons of the oil in the skillet.

4. Add the chopped onion to the skillet. Lower the heat to low and sauté for about 5 minutes, until the onion is soft and somewhat golden.

5. Add the sliced mushrooms to the skillet. Saute for 10 minutes, stirring often, until the mushrooms are nicely browned. Add the minced garlic and sauté for 1 or 2 minutes. Add the oregano, the salt, and the pepper. Add the tomato sauce and the sausage meat. Stir well and simmer for 5 minutes.

6. By now the pasta water should be boiling. Cook the pasta according to package directions. (You can let the sauce simmer over low heat.)

7. When the pasta is "al dente," drain, place in a serving bowl, add the sauce and mix well. Have extra Parmesan cheese available at the table.

Goes well with:

- Drinks: red wine, like Chianti, Primitivo (which is the Italian for Zinfandel) or a Pinot Noir. If you are feeling more adventurous try a "Dolcetto" or a "Rosso di Montalcino."
- Other recipes: serve with crusty bread; this recipe is a meal in itself.

Notes/Evaluation:

Spaghetti with Gorgonzola & Walnuts (V)

Equipment needed:

colander

Special notes:

Gorgonzola is an Italian blue-veined cheese. Since this sauce depends on the flavor of this cheese, buy a good one from a cheese shop. You may, however, substitute blue cheese (which is substantially milder and less flavorful), or some other cheese (such as Roquefort, Stilton, or other creamy type), or you can even mix half the Gorgonzola with an equal amount of cream cheese. You can also make a paste of the Gorgonzola by adding a tablespoon or so of milk, or of hot pasta water.

Ingredients:

- 1 pound spaghetti

- 6 tablespoons olive oil
- 2 garlic cloves, minced
- 1/4 cup walnuts, minced
- 4 ounces Gorgonzola, crumbled and softened to room temperature

Instructions:

1. In a pan of boiling salted water cook the pasta according to package directions. Cook "al dente" – firm to the bite, not mushy.
2. While the water is boiling, heat the oil in a skillet over low to medium heat. Sauté the garlic for about 1 or 2 minutes, till golden brown. Do not burn.
3. Add the walnuts and sauté for 2 to 3 minutes, stirring well.
4. When the pasta is cooked, drain, place in a serving bowl, add the oil-garlic mixture and the Gorgonzola, and mix well. Serve.

Goes well with:

- Drinks: hearty red wine.
- Other recipes: salad; crusty bread; chicken.

Notes/Evaluation:

Spaghetti with Salsa Fresca (V)

Equipment needed:

colander
pepper grinder

Special notes:

This is one of my favorite sauces for spaghetti, especially when the weather is warm (in Arizona that's most of the time!). Strangely enough, you do not cook this sauce. The "salsa" is in this case the Italian word, not the Mexican one, so no jalapenos or cilantro are involved.

Ingredients:

- 1 pound of spaghetti (or linguine)
- 4 large tomatoes, minced
- 2 cloves garlic minced
- 1 small onion minced
- 1 teaspoon dried basil (or 8 to 10 fresh leaves)
- 1/2 teaspoon dried rosemary
- 1/2 teaspoon dried oregano
- 1/2 teaspoon salt
- 1 teaspoon freshly ground black pepper
- 1/2 cup olive oil
- 1 lemon, juice only (or the equivalent bottled)
- grated Parmesan cheese, for serving at the table

Instructions:

1. In a large bowl mix all the ingredients listed (except the spaghetti and the cheese). If you are using any fresh herbs, like the basil, rosemary, or oregano, wash and dry them, and mince them. If you are using dried herbs, when you place them in the bowl, rub them between your thumb and finger to release the flavor.
2. Let the bowl sit at room temperature for 2-3 hours or more so the flavors will blend (cover with plastic wrap).
3. Prepare the spaghetti using the directions on the package.
4. Serve the spaghetti in a bowl, topped with a generous serving of the sauce. Have additional sauce and grated cheese available at the table.

Goes well with:

- Drinks: any red wine such as Pinot Noir.
- Other recipes: French bread; salad.

Notes/Evaluation:

Spaghetti with Sausage

Equipment needed:

frying pan
large saucepan
colander

Special notes:

This is a slightly different version of the Spaghetti alla Puttanesca.

Ingredients:

- 1 lb. Sausage, mild or hot (preferably from deli), sliced into 1/2-inch thick slices
- 1 tablespoon olive oil
- 5 garlic cloves, cut into pieces
- 5 tablespoons olive oil
- 2 cans of Italian tomatoes (large, about 28 oz. each; plum or stewed tomatoes)
- 2 cups pitted black olives (medium or large size), sliced
- 2 tablespoons capers
- 1 can anchovies, minced
- 1/2 cup fresh parsley, minced
- 1 tablespoon dried oregano
- 1/2 teaspoon salt
- 1/2 teaspoon freshly ground pepper

Instructions:

1. Heat 1 tablespoon olive oil over low to medium heat and sauté sausage until brown (about 7 to 10 minutes). If necessary increase or lower the heat so as not to burn the sausage. Stir frequently. When done place sausage on paper towels on a dish and set aside.
2. In same pan sauté garlic in 5 tablespoons of olive oil (less if there's oil from the sausage), until the garlic is soft. Use medium to low heat so garlic won't burn. Discard garlic.
3. To same pan add tomatoes (if they seem watery, drain some of the liquid), olives, and capers. Cook over medium high heat for 10 minutes, stirring frequently, until sauce thickens.
4. Bring to boil water in a large (6- or 8-quart) saucepan and cook spaghetti according to package directions (usually 10 to 12 minutes).
5. While spaghetti cooks, add anchovies, parsley, oregano, and sausage to tomato sauce. Cook for another 10 to 15 minutes over medium heat. Season to taste with salt and pepper.
6. Drain spaghetti and spoon sauce over them.

Goes well with:

- Drinks: red wine.
- Other recipes: garlic toast; a salad.

Ziti with Broccoli (V)

Equipment needed:

heavy skillet
colander

Special notes:

Excellent taste and healthy too (except for the butter...).

Ingredients:

- 2 sticks butter
- 2 large garlic cloves, cut in half
- salt and pepper
- 1/2 teaspoon dry basil
- 1/2 teaspoon dry oregano
- 1/2 to 1 bunch fresh broccoli (discard stems & clean)
- 1/4 cup ricotta
- 1 pound ziti

Instructions:

1. In a heavy skillet over low to medium heat melt the butter. Add the garlic, salt and pepper to taste, basil and oregano, mix, and leave on low heat.
2. Cook the broccoli in a pot of boiling salted water. The broccoli is ready when it can be easily pierced with a fork. Better to be undercooked and crunchy than overcooked and mushy. Drain and cut into bite size pieces. Add to the butter sauce.
3. Cook the ziti in a pot of boiling water, following the package directions. Drain well with colander.
4. Place the ziti in a large bowl and toss with the ricotta cheese. Pour the broccoli and butter sauce over the ziti. Mix well and serve.

Goes well with:

- Drinks: a hearty red wine.
- Other recipes: salad; French bread; ice cream for dessert.

Notes/Evaluation:

Rice & Polenta

Chinese Fried Rice

Equipment needed:

wok

Special notes:

This recipe is fairly basic. You can add more ingredients like cooked shrimp or chicken (these should be pre-cooked and small), or some other vegetables like green beans, broccoli, or mushrooms (all finely diced).

Ingredients:

- 4 cups cold cooked rice
- 3 tablespoons vegetable oil
- 4 eggs (whisked together with the salt)
- 1/2 teaspoon salt
- 1 cup diced cooked ham
- 1/2 cup canned peas
- 1 carrot, peeled and finely diced
- 2 tablespoons chopped green onions
- soy sauce (optional)

Instructions:

1. Cook the rice according to package directions. Set aside and let cool (can be done the day ahead).
2. Have all your ingredients ready.
3. Heat the wok over medium-high heat. When hot add one tablespoon of the vegetable oil and swirl the oil all around the wok's surface by rotating the wok (use pot handles to hold on to the wok, as the handles get hot).
4. Add the eggs and stir well with a spoon; as they cook break them up into small pieces.
5. Remove the eggs to a bowl.
6. Add 2 tablespoons vegetable oil to the wok and let the oil get hot. Again, swirl the oil around the wok's surface.
7. Add the cooked rice, the ham, peas, and carrot and stir well.
8. Add the cooked eggs, the chopped green onion, and stir well.
9. Remove from heat and serve on a platter or bowl. If you like, have some soy sauce available.

Goes well with:

- Drinks: hot tea.
- Other recipes: a chicken dish like Jerusalem-style chicken.

Notes/Evaluation:

Chinese Rice (V)

Equipment needed:

pan

Special notes:

A quickie recipe

Ingredients:

- 1 package of "instant" rice
- 1/2 cup green onions, thinly sliced
- 4 tablespoons butter
- 1 teaspoon white pepper

Instructions:

1. Prepare the rice according to package directions.
2. Place the cooked rice in a bowl, add the other three ingredients, and mix well.
3. Voila! Wasn't that simple?

Goes well with:

- Drinks: beer; a dry white wine like Chablis.
- Other recipes: sautéed vegetables.

Notes/Evaluation:

RICE & POLENTA

Polenta (V)

Equipment needed:

a heavy pan
a small pan
a long wooden-handled spoon

Special notes:

Polenta is an ethnic dish from Northern Italy. It is essentially corn mush, but don't let that description deter you. It is quite delicious and versatile. You can serve it as a main dish, covered with your favorite spaghetti sauce, or with soft cheese like a mixture of cream cheese and blue cheese, or you can have it at breakfast covered with pancake syrup.

Ingredients:

- 2 cups corn meal
- 1 tablespoon vegetable oil
- water
- salt

Instructions:

1. In a heavy pan mix the corn meal with the vegetable oil and with cold water from the faucet, to make a paste. This step is very much like mixing cement. Add the water a little at a time and keep mixing till you have a smooth paste. Since different brands of corn meal have different consistencies, it is difficult to specify how much water you need.

2. In another pan, place several cups of water to heat on the stove. Then place the heavy pan on the stove and cook the corn meal, stirring continuously for about 1/2 hour. As you stir add a little bit of the hot water so you always have a smooth paste. In particular break up any globs, make sure the polenta doesn't burn at the bottom of the pan, and continue mixing. For best results use a long-handled wooden spoon. As you stir add a bit of salt to taste.

3. Once you have achieved a well-mixed, smooth paste, dump the polenta into a bowl, and let it sit for 3 to 5 minutes. It should be fairly solid.

4. Place a dish bottom side up on top of the bowl and turn the bowl over, so the polenta plops onto the dish (Do this carefully, and over a clean counter just in case…).

5. Slice (or scoop) the polenta onto dishes and top with hot spaghetti sauce or melted cheese.

Goes well with:

- Drinks: robust red wines like a hearty burgundy, Pinot Noir, Merlot, etc.
- Other recipes: sautéed vegetables, like mushrooms.

Notes/Evaluation:

Polenta with Ham

Equipment needed:

whisk
baking dish about 8 X 12 inches

Special notes:

Polenta is a very popular Italian dish. Like pasta, it is served with something in it or on it. In fact you can use spaghetti sauce, mushrooms, sausage, gorgonzola (blue cheese), and a variety of other ingredients. Once you've mastered the technique of making polenta, try your hand at adding other ingredients. This recipe is somewhat unusual in that most of the cooking of the polenta is done in the oven. Ordinarily, polenta is stirred continuously over heat (as in the previous recipe).

Ingredients:

- 3 cups milk
- 1/8 teaspoon ground nutmeg
- 1/4 teaspoon freshly ground pepper
- 1/2 teaspoon salt
- 1-1/2 cups yellow cornmeal
- 1-1/2 cups diced ham
- 1 cup grated Parmesan cheese
- 2 tablespoons butter

Instructions:

1. In a heavy large pan mix the milk with the nutmeg, pepper, and salt and bring to a boil over medium heat.
2. Preheat the oven to 450 degrees.
3. Whisk in the cornmeal a little at a time until the mixture is thick and smooth.
4. Mix in the ham and the Parmesan cheese. Remove from the heat and pour the polenta into a buttered oven-proof baking dish (about 8 X 12). Add the two tablespoons of butter in small dots over the surface.
5. Bake the polenta in the oven until the top begins to brown (about 25 to 35 minutes).
6. Remove from oven and let sit for a few minutes. Cut into slices and serve.

Goes well with:

- Drinks: red wine like a Sangiovese.
- Other recipes: very good as an accompaniment to a vegetable medley.

Notes/Evaluation:

Rice and Beef Teriyaki

Equipment needed:
wok

Special notes:
Teriyaki cooking involves marinading the meat and serving it with vegetables or other ingredients.

Ingredients:
For the marinade (skip if you use a bottled marinade):
- 1 tablespoon dry sherry
- 3 tablespoons soy sauce
- 1-1/2 teaspoons garlic powder
- 1 teaspoon ground ginger
- 1 pound boneless steak (flank steak or better cuts of meat)
- 1/4 head cauliflower
- 4 carrots
- 1 cup chopped Bok Choy (Chinese cabbage)
- 1 cup rice
- 1 cup beef broth (canned or made from cubes)
- 1 tablespoon peanut oil
- 4 teaspoons cornstarch

Instructions:
1. Prepare the marinade by mixing all the ingredients (from sherry through ginger) in a medium size bowl (or use a commercially prepared marinade).
2. Slice the meat into thin slices (about the thickness of two nickels; meat is easier to slice if it is partly frozen). Place the sliced meat in the marinade, and marinate for 1 hour or more in the refrigerator. You can use a bowl or a 1-gallon plastic bag (make sure the bag doesn't leak). Stir occasionally, so all the slices of meat get coated.
3. Clean the vegetables and cut into bite size pieces. For the cauliflower use the flowerets only, not the stems.
4. Prepare the rice according to the package directions.
5. Heat the broth.
6. Heat the wok. When it is hot, add the peanut oil and swirl the wok, so most of the surface gets coated with the oil.
7. Stir fry the meat in the wok until the meat is browned (about 2 minutes).
8. Add the vegetables and stir fry until tender but still crisp – about 3 minutes.

9. Mix the cornstarch into the hot broth, and gently pour the broth into the wok. Let the broth boil for about 1 minute and stir.

10. Remove the wok from the heat, mix in the rice, and serve on a platter or individual dishes.

Goes well with:
- Drinks: tea; beer; mineral water with a slice of lemon; white dry wine.
- Other recipes: a meal in itself; could go with a salad.

Notes/Evaluation:

Rice with Mid-Eastern Sauce (V)

Special notes:

This is a good sauce to use over chicken breasts or pork chops. Most if not all of the ingredients are available in a supermarket; you might need to get cooked figs at a mid-Eastern deli.

Ingredients:

- rice (follow package directions for 4)
- 1 cup dry white whine (like Chardonnay)
- 1/2 cup soy sauce
- 1/2 stick unsalted butter
- 4 tablespoons all purpose flour
- 1 lime – grate the rind
- 1/2 cup lime juice (fresh or bottled)
- 1 onion minced
- 1 teaspoon dried thyme
- 1 teaspoon dried oregano
- 1 teaspoon curry powder
- 1 teaspoon ground ginger
- 1 cup cooked figs (in a jar)
- 1 tablespoon honey
- 1/4 teaspoon salt

Instructions:

1. Cook the rice according to package directions; this usually involves boiling water, adding the rice, and cooking for 20 minutes.
2. In a saucepan combine the wine and the soy sauce and heat over low medium heat. In a second saucepan melt the butter over low heat. When it is melted, add the flour and mix well.
3. Add the wine-soy sauce mixture to the butter and mix over medium heat, till the sauce thickens. Add all the other ingredients and mix well.
4. You can pour the sauce directly over the rice or let each guest pour their own.

Goes well with:

- Drinks: hot tea; mineral water with a slice of lemon; white wine.
- Other recipes: good accompaniment for sautéed vegetables or a chicken dish.

Notes/Evaluation:

Rice with Sauteed Mixed Vegetables (V)

Equipment needed:

pepper grinder (optional)

Special notes:

Rice, like pasta, goes well with a variety of other foods, and is easy to prepare.

Ingredients:

- 1 cup rice (follow package directions for cooking)
- 2 tablespoons olive oil
- 1 tablespoon anchovy paste (you can use anchovy fillets)
- 1 onion, minced
- 2 zucchinis, sliced thin crosswise (little discs)
- 2 small summer (yellow) squash, sliced thin crosswise
- 2 carrots, sliced thin crosswise
- 1 Bok Choy (Chinese cabbage) or other cabbage, sliced into small pieces (about 4 cups)
- 2 tablespoons rice (or white) vinegar
- 1/2 teaspoon salt
- 1/2 teaspoon freshly ground pepper
- 1 tablespoon dried oregano

Instructions:

1. Prepare all the vegetables by cleaning them and slicing.
2. Cook the rice according to package directions.
3. While the rice is cooking, heat the oil and the anchovy paste in a large skillet that will hold all the vegetables, over medium heat. Add the onion and sauté until golden.
4. Add the other vegetables except for the Bok Choy cabbage and sauté for 5 minutes, stirring often. Add the Bok Choy, vinegar, salt, pepper, and oregano, and sauté for another 5 minutes, while stirring. The vegetables should be crisp, not limp.
5. Serve on a platter; you can place the rice on a separate dish, or on the platter next to the vegetables.

Goes well with:

- Drinks: a light "bubbly" type of red wine like Lambrusco, Riunite brand wine, or a Beaujolais.
- Other recipes: this is a meal in itself; goes well with crusty bread.

Notes/Evaluation:

Risotto (V)

Equipment needed:
- a ladle
- a heavy pan

Special notes:

I was born in Torino in northern Italy, a region that is the center of rice cultivation, and risotto there is what pasta is to the rest of Italy – indispensable and to die for. You will need Arborio rice, available in many supermarkets and specialty stores. If you can, buy the Parmesan cheese at a cheese shop and ask for Parmigiano-Reggiano. As with pasta, you can add a lot of different ingredients, from seafood (e.g., small shrimp), to cheese (Gorgonzola), even fruit (e.g., pears). The next three recipes are some examples.

Ingredients:
- 8 cups of chicken broth (or vegetarian; canned or bouillon)
- 2 tablespoons olive oil
- 1 yellow onion, finely minced
- 2-1/2 cups Arborio rice
- 1 cup grated Parmesan cheese

Instructions:

1. In a medium size pan bring the broth to a boil, and then reduce the heat so it simmers.
2. In a heavy pan heat the olive oil over medium heat. Then add the onion and cook for about 3 to 5 minutes, stirring occasionally.
3. Increase the heat to high and put the rice in the pan. Cook, stirring, for about 1 or 2 minutes, until the rice is mixed with the olive oil.
4. Reduce the heat to low and add to the rice 3 ladles of the simmering broth. Stir the mixture. When the rice has absorbed most of the liquid, add a ladle of the broth and continue stirring. Continue this procedure of ladling the broth as the rice absorbs the liquid. You will also need to increase the heat slightly so the rice continues to cook at a steady pace. The rice should be ready in about 20 to 25 minutes. As in cooking pasta, you will need to taste it and make sure it is "al dente," cooked but not mushy. If you run out of broth simply use a bit of hot water.
5. When the risotto is ready, add the cheese and stir it well.
6. Serve, either directly from the pan, in a serving bowl, or in individual dishes.

Goes well with:
- Drinks: any red wine, especially light ones like a Gamay Beaujolais.
- Other recipes: a meal in itself; serve with crusty bread; a small side salad.

Notes/Evaluation:

Risotto with Mushrooms (V)

Special notes:

Here is a variation of the basic risotto recipe. If you can find fresh porcini mushrooms use those (they have a stronger flavor); otherwise you can use dried porcini mushrooms (just soak them in lukewarm water), or white button mushrooms.

Ingredients:

- see recipe for risotto

- 4 tablespoons olive oil
- 1 garlic clove minced
- 3/4 pound mushrooms, thinly sliced
- 1 tablespoon chopped fresh basil
- 4 tablespoons chopped parsley
- 1/2 teaspoon salt
- 1/4 teaspoon freshly ground pepper

Instructions:

1. First follow the basic recipe for risotto. When you get to step 4 of the risotto, you can prepare the mushrooms, as you keep an eye on the risotto.

2. In a skillet, heat the olive oil over medium heat. Add the minced garlic and sauté for a couple of minutes.

3. Add the mushrooms, basil, parsley, salt, and pepper and cook over medium to medium-high heat, stirring occasionally. It should take about 7 to 10 minutes for the mushrooms to be ready. If necessary, set the mushrooms aside.

4. Go back to the risotto recipe. In step 5 when you add the cheese, also add the mushrooms and mix well (if you prefer, you could serve the mushrooms separately).

5. Serve directly from the pan, or from a serving dish.

Goes well with:

- Drinks: any red wine.
- Other recipes: a meal in itself, but could be served with a salad, and/or as a side dish to chicken, or a vegetable medley.

Notes/Evaluation:

RICE & POLENTA

Risotto with Red Wine (V)

Special notes:

Risotto is a very popular dish in Italy, particularly in the north, where there are extensive rice fields. For risotto, you need to use Arborio rice, which is available in gourmet shops and other stores. You can buy the broth in cans or waxed-paper containers, or you can easily make your own by using bouillon cubes. If you want a vegetarian dish, use vegetable broth – otherwise, use chicken broth.

Ingredients:

- 6 cups broth (vegetarian or chicken; canned or Bouillon)
- 2 tablespoons olive oil
- 1 yellow onion, finely minced
- 2-1/2 cups Arborio rice
- 2 cups red wine (like a Chianti)
- 1 cup grated Parmesan cheese

Instructions:

1. In a medium size pan bring the broth to a boil, and then reduce the heat so it simmers.
2. In a heavy pan heat the olive oil over medium heat. Then add the onion and cook for about 3 to 5 minutes, stirring occasionally.
3. Increase the heat to high and put the rice in the pan. Cook, stirring, for about 1 or 2 minutes, until the rice is coated with the olive oil.
4. Reduce the heat to low and add about 3 ladles of the simmering broth. Stir the mixture. When the rice has absorbed most of the liquid, add the wine, and stir. When that has been absorbed, continue adding the broth a ladle at a time. Always wait to add broth until the liquid in the pan has been absorbed by the rice. You might need to increase the heat a bit, so the rice continues to cook at a steady pace. Conversely, as you remove the broth from the first pan, you might need to lower that heat, so the broth does not boil.
5. The rice should be ready in about 20 to 25 minutes. As in cooking pasta you will need to taste it, and make sure it is "al dente" – cooked but not mushy. If it looks like you will run out of broth before the rice is ready, heat more broth, or if absolutely necessary use a bit of hot water.

6. When the risotto is ready you can add the cheese directly to the pan and stir it well, or you can serve the cheese separately.
7. Serve directly from the pan, or from a bowl, or place directly on individual dishes.

Goes well with:
- Drinks: use the same wine you used in the recipe.
- Other recipes: this is a meal in itself, but you can serve a salad, or serve the risotto as a first course followed by chicken, meat, fish, vegetables, etc.

Notes/Evaluation:

Risotto with Pesto (V)

Special notes:

You can combine recipes or portions of recipes to obtain a new dish. This is a good example.

Ingredients:

- You will need the ingredients for the risotto as listed in the risotto recipe, and the ingredients for the pesto sauce as listed in the Linguine with Pesto recipe.

Instructions:

1. See the recipe for Linguine al Pesto in the pasta section, and follow the first two steps to make the pesto sauce.
2. Now see the recipe for risotto and follow it. When you get to step 5 add the pesto sauce (about 6 tablespoons) and the cheese and stir well.
3. Serve.

Goes well with:

- Drinks: any red wine – try a Bardolino or a Barolo.
- Other recipes: a meal in itself; or serve as a first course followed by a chicken recipe or a vegetable medley.

Notes/Evaluation:

Vegetables

Bagna Cauda (Vegetables with Hot Oil) (V)

Equipment needed:

fondue pot
long handled (fondue) forks
pepper grinder

Special notes:

This is the Italian equivalent of fondue, and an excellent way to eat lots of vegetables. It is very simple to prepare, and makes a wonderful meal. Good etiquette requires two forks per person – the long handled fork to dip the vegetables in the communal pot, and a regular fork to eat with.

Ingredients:

- Crisp clean vegetables cut into bite size pieces. My favorite include: cauliflower; carrots; bell peppers (especially red and yellow); zucchinis; mushrooms; fennel; celery; and turnips.

- 1/2 cup olive oil
- 1/4 pound butter
- 1 can anchovy fillets, minced
- 6 garlic cloves, minced
- freshly ground black pepper
- 1 or 2 loaves of crusty French bread

Instructions:

1. Prepare all the vegetables and arrange on a serving platter.
2. In the fondue pot combine the olive oil and the butter. Cook over low heat and stir, until the butter has melted.
3. Add the anchovies, garlic, and pepper and simmer for about 10 minutes.
4. Bring the pot to the table, light the candle or Sterno underneath to keep the contents simmering. To eat, spear a piece of vegetable with a long-handled fork and dip into the pot (use a stirring motion so you will coat the vegetable piece with anchovy). Use pieces of crusty bread to bring the dipped vegetable to your dish, to avoid spills and burns. Once the dipped vegetable is on your dish, use your regular fork to eat it.
5. As you eat, experiment leaving pieces of vegetables to cook longer in the oil. Don't however, overcook them or they won't taste that good.

Goes well with:

- Drinks: a hearty red wine.
- Other recipes: this is a meal in itself, but you must have the crusty French (or Italian) bread.

Notes/Evaluation:

VEGETABLES

Carrots with Cheese

Equipment needed:

peeler
oven-proof baking dish

Special notes:

If you can, buy organically grown carrots that have not been sprayed with insecticide. Buy individual carrots (not bags) that are orange, with bright green leaves, not rubbery, and with no cracks. Fontina cheese has a wonderful flavor; buy it at a cheese shop.

Ingredients:

- 10 carrots, peeled and cut into 2-inch segments
- 1/2 cup grated Fontina cheese
- 4 tablespoons grated Parmesan cheese
- 2 tablespoons bread crumbs
- 1/4 cup melted butter

Instructions:

1. Fill a medium size pan with water and bring it to a boil over high heat. As you wait for the water to boil, do steps 2, 3, 4, and 5.
2. Preheat the oven to 425 degrees.
3. Clean and peel the carrots, and cut into 2-inch segments.
4. Have an oven-proof baking dish large enough to hold the carrots, and grease it well with either butter or Crisco.
5. In a small pan place a stick of butter and let it melt over low heat.
6. When the water is boiling, drop the carrots in for 8 minutes. Drain.
7. Place the carrots in the greased baking pan, and sprinkle the cheeses, bread crumbs, and melted butter over them.
8. Bake in the oven for about 5 minutes, or until the cheeses have melted and are golden brown.
9. Serve.

Goes well with:

- Drinks: depends on the main dish.
- Other recipes: any meat or chicken dish (that does not have cheese in it).

Notes/Evaluation:

Chiles Rellenos (Stuffed Chili Peppers) (V)

Equipment needed:

oven-proof baking dish

Special notes:

There are a lot of ways to fix chiles rellenos, a traditional Mexican dish. All of them basically involve stuffing the peppers (not always with cheese) and frying them in batter. Here is a slightly different version.

Ingredients:

- 8 fresh green chilies
- 1 pound Monterey Jack cheese, shredded
- 4 eggs
- 1/2 teaspoon salt
- 1/2 teaspoon pepper
- 3 tablespoons all purpose flour
- 1/4 cup vegetable oil (like corn)
- 1 cup Taco sauce (or Mexican salsa)
- 2 cups shredded lettuce
- 1 can refried beans (vegetarian style)
- 1 bag of tortilla chips (optional)

Instructions:

1. Wash and dry the chilies.
2. Make a slit along one side of each chili to open it up. Do it gently so they don't tear at the stem. Clean out the seeds (you can tap gently on the chile with a knife handle to shake the seeds out).
3. Stuff the chilies with cheese. There should be cheese left over for steps 9 and 10.
4. Separate the eggs and beat the whites until stiff.
5. Beat the yolks and fold into the whites, together with the salt, pepper, and flour.
6. Heat the oil in a large skillet over medium heat. Also begin heating your broiler (needed for step #9).
7. While the oil is heating, heat the Taco sauce in one pan and the refried beans in another (use medium heat).
8. Place the stuffed chilies into the hot oil (careful!) and fry until golden brown. Be careful; if oil is too hot, chilies will burn.
9. Place chilies in a oven-proof baking pan, add some cheese as a topping and heat under the broiler to melt the cheese.
10. Add some shredded cheese to the refried beans and mix in; let it melt.

11. Place 2 chilies on each individual dish, top with some of the warm taco sauce (or salsa), and place some shredded lettuce and some refried beans on side of dish. Serve with tortilla chips.

Goes well with:

- Drinks: cold beer (one of my favorites is Negra Modelo); margaritas.
- Other recipes: this is a meal in itself.

Notes/Evaluation:

Chiles Rellenos with Pico de Gallo Sauce (V)

Equipment needed:
electric (or hand) beater
slotted spoon (optional)

Special notes:
Tucson has an abundance of great Mexican restaurants, and many serve excellent chiles rellenos. This is a main dish in itself.

Ingredients:
For the Pico de Gallo sauce:
- 2 tomatoes, finely diced
- 1 red onion, finely diced
- 4 tablespoons lemon juice (2 lemons)
- 2 tablespoons minced fresh cilantro
- 1 jalapeno (or Serrano) chile, seeded and finely diced
- 1 tablespoon olive oil
- 1/4 teaspoon salt
- 1/4 teaspoon freshly ground pepper

- 8 green chilies, preferably fresh (use mild ones like poblanos)
- 1 pound Monterey Jack cheese or mild cheddar cheese, shredded
- 2 scallions, minced finely (use mostly white part)
- 3 eggs, at room temperature
- 2 tablespoons all purpose flour
- 1 teaspoon salt
- 1 teaspoon pepper

Instructions:
1. Place the peppers underneath a broiler and turn occasionally until they are blackened on all sides (about 10 minutes).
2. Place the peppers in a brown paper bag, seal the bag, and wait till they are cool enough to handle. Peel the charred shin from the peppers, and discard.
3. Make the Pico de Gallo sauce by mixing well all the ingredients in a bowl. Be careful when you seed and dice the jalapeno or Serrano chili. Wear rubber gloves (or plastic bags held at the wrist by rubber bands).
4. In a separate bowl, mix the scallions and the cheese.
5. Make a long slit on the side of each pepper and remove the seeds. Handle carefully, so the whole pepper does not fall apart. Fill the peppers with the cheese and scallion mixture.
6. In a large skillet heat the vegetable oil over medium heat. While the oil is heating, separate the eggs and place the yolks in one bowl and the whites in another. Add 1/4 teaspoon salt to the whites.
7. In a bowl using an electric (or hand) beater, beat the egg whites and salt until stiff. In a separate bowl beat the yolks, and fold the yolks into the whites, and gently mix in the flour, salt, and pepper.

8. Dip the stuffed chilies, one at a time, into the egg batter and coat the chili well. Then place each coated chile into the hot oil (careful, it may spatter). You can probably fit only 3 or 4 chiles in the skillet, so you'll do this in batches.

9. Cook the chilies until they are golden brown on all sides (you'll need to turn them over with a slotted spoon).

10. Serve the chilies in individual dishes with the Pico de Gallo sauce.

Goes well with:
- Drinks: ice cold beer.
- Other recipes: refried beans; Mexican rice; tortillas; shredded lettuce.

Notes/Evaluation:

Eggplant Medley with Mint Dressing (V)

Equipment needed:

colander
vegetable brush
vegetable peeler

Special notes:

This is a very nice vegetable medley that can be prepared ahead, and in fact tastes better as a leftover. When buying the eggplants and the other vegetables, make sure they are firm and unblemished.

Ingredients:

- 2 small eggplants
- 1/2 teaspoon salt
- 3 medium zucchinis, diced into small pieces
- 2 bell peppers, diced into small pieces
- 4 tablespoons olive oil

For the dressing:
- 3 garlic cloves, minced in 1/2 teaspoon salt
- 3 tablespoons white vinegar
- 1/2 teaspoon dried mint
- 1/2 teaspoon dried basil
- 1/2 teaspoon dried oregano
- 1/2 teaspoon dried marjoram
- 1 tablespoon freshly chopped parsley
- 6 tablespoons olive oil
- 1/2 teaspoon salt
- 1/2 teaspoon freshly ground black pepper

Instructions:

1. Peel the eggplants using the vegetable peeler, cut into small cubes (about the size of your fingernail), place in the colander, and sprinkle with the salt. Let stand for 30 minutes in the sink. Sometimes, eggplants have a bitter taste, and the salt draws the bitter liquid out. If the eggplants are not bitter, sprinkling with salt is not necessary.

2. Prepare the garlic cloves by mincing with 1/2 teaspoon of salt to form a paste. In a large bowl mix the garlic with the vinegar and the five spices listed above. As you place each dry spice in the bowl, crumble it with your fingers to release the flavor. Add the 6 tablespoons of olive oil and mix well with a fork or whisk. Set aside.

3. Prepare the zucchinis and the bell peppers. To clean the zucchinis scrub them with the brush, pat dry, and dice. The bell peppers need only to be washed; then pat dry and dice.

4. Rinse the eggplant cubes under cold water (if you used salt in step #1), and gently pat dry.

5. In a large skillet heat 2 tablespoons of oil over moderate heat. When the oil is hot, cook the bell peppers for 5 minutes. Add 2 more tablespoons of oil, the eggplant cubes, and cook for 10 minutes, stirring often.
6. Add the zucchinis, cook for 10 more minutes, and stir frequently.
7. Toss the warm vegetables with the dressing in a large bowl, and let the mixture reach room temperature. Before serving, season with salt and freshly ground black pepper.

Goes well with:
- Drinks: red wine.
- Other recipes: this recipe can be used as a main dish, as an accompaniment to a main dish of chicken or pasta, or as an appetizer.

Notes/Evaluation:

Garlic Mushrooms (V)

Equipment needed:
egg slicer to slice the mushrooms

Special notes:
A very simple and fast recipe

Ingredients:
- 2 pounds white mushrooms, cleaned and sliced
- 2 tablespoons olive oil
- 2 tablespoons butter
- 6 garlic cloves, minced
- 1/2 teaspoon salt
- 1/2 teaspoon freshly ground pepper
- 1 tablespoon chopped parsley or basil (optional)

Instructions:
1. Clean the mushrooms by wiping each with a damp paper towel. Cut off the lowest portion of the stem (about a dime size slice) and discard. Slice the mushrooms by using the egg slicer.
2. Melt the oil and the butter in a large skillet over medium high heat. When the butter foams add the mushrooms.
3. Sauté over high heat, stirring frequently, until the mushrooms are golden.
4. Add the garlic, salt, and pepper and sauté for about 2 minutes longer. If you want, you can add the chopped parsley or chopped basil at this time.

Goes well with:
- Drinks: anything, depending on the main course.
- Other recipes: just about any meat or chicken recipe that doesn't already have mushrooms in it.

Notes/Evaluation:

Italian Broccoli (V)

Equipment needed:
colander to drain the broccoli

Special notes:
From a health point of view, broccoli is excellent. If you're not too crazy about broccoli, this recipe just might change your mind.

Ingredients:
- 2 pounds or more of broccoli
- 2 tablespoons of salt
- 4 tablespoons olive oil
- 2 tablespoons fresh lemon juice (1 lemon)
- 1/2 teaspoon salt
- 1/2 teaspoon freshly ground pepper

Instructions:
1. Fill a 6-quart pot (or larger) about 2/3 with water and bring to a boil. When the water boils add 2 tablespoons of salt.
2. Meanwhile, clean the broccoli under cold water. Remove the major portion of the stalks and discard; separate the flowerets into bite size or larger portions.
3. When the water boils, place the broccoli flowerets in the pot and cook for about 4 minutes. The broccoli should be crisp and not mushy.
4. Drain, and place the broccoli on a serving platter.
5. Drizzle the olive oil, lemon juice, salt, and pepper.
6. Let it cool. Best served at room temperature or on the cold side (even better the next day).

Goes well with:
- Drinks: depends on the main course.
- Other recipes: goes well with chicken or meat recipes.

Notes/Evaluation:

Italian Vegetables (V)

Special notes:

As a child in Italy, I lived on a farm for a while to escape World War II bombardments. Something similar to this recipe was served quite often, when the food was available. Basically, you can treat this dish as a salad; if you want to add other condiments, go ahead, or if you have a favorite bottled salad dressing, use that. I like to use rice vinegar or red wine vinegar, but any vinegar will do. This is a meal in itself, or can be used as a side dish.

Ingredients:

- 1 head cauliflower
- 3 broccoli stalks
- 6 carrots
- 1 tablespoon of salt
- 1/2 pound olives (Kalamata or whatever you like)

For the dressing:

- 4 tablespoons olive oil
- 6 tablespoons rice vinegar (or other type)
- 2 tablespoons lemon juice (1 lemon)
- 1 teaspoon dried oregano
- 1 teaspoon freshly ground pepper

Instructions:

1. Heat to boiling a large (6-quart) pot of water (about 2/3 full).
2. While the water is heating, clean the vegetables and cut into small pieces, about 2 to 3 times bite size. Do not use the large part of the broccoli stalk or the core of the cauliflower.
3. When the water boils add one tablespoon of salt, and then add the three vegetables. Heat for 5 minutes and drain.
4. Place the drained vegetables in a large platter or bowl. Add the olives and sprinkle the last 5 ingredients of the dressing, and toss gently but well (if you wanted to, you could mix the five ingredients for the dressing in a jar).
5. Cover with foil or plastic wrap and let stand at room temperature. Toss before serving.

Goes well with:

- Drinks: red wine; iced tea; mineral water.
- Other recipes: this is a meal in itself; serve with crusty bread.

Notes/Evaluation:

Marinated Beets (V)

Equipment needed:

whisk (or use fork)
scrubbing brush

Special notes:

A tasty cold vegetable that can be used as an appetizer, part of a buffet, or a side dish.

Ingredients:

- 6 to 8 beets (preferably fresh, or two cans)
- 2 tablespoons olive oil
- 3 tablespoons lemon juice
- 2 garlic cloves, minced
- 1/4 teaspoon, or more, of salt
- 1/4 teaspoon dried oregano
- 1/2 teaspoon freshly ground pepper
- 3 green onions, white part only, minced
- 1 tablespoon parsley, minced

Instructions:

(If you use canned beets, go to step #3)

1. Heat a pan of water on the stove. While the water is heating, clean the beets under cold water with a scrubbing brush. Place the beets in the pan of hot water and simmer until tender – about 40 to 45 minutes.
2. Remove pan from heat, take beets out of the pan and let cool. When they are cool, peel them, and slice thinly.
3. Make the marinade by whisking together the olive oil and lemon juice, and add the garlic, salt, oregano, and pepper.
4. Place the beet slices in a bowl and toss gently with the marinade. Place bowl in refrigerator for half an hour or more.
5. Before serving, add green onions, and toss gently. Sprinkle parsley on top.

Goes well with:

- Drinks: red wine.
- Other recipes: crusty bread.

Notes/Evaluation:

Moroccan Vegetables (V)

Equipment needed:

oven-proof baking pan with lid (if no lid, use foil)

Special notes:

I am partial to Moroccan cuisine because of the spices used. Try this recipe as a good example. The dish is ready when the potatoes are; to test, use a fork – the potato should be "fluffy" rather than hard (you can also do a taste test).

Ingredients:

- 2 tablespoons olive oil
- 1 tablespoon minced garlic cloves (about 4 or 5)
- 1 onion diced
- 1 cup vegetable broth (or chicken)
- 1 teaspoon ground ginger
- 1/2 teaspoon cayenne pepper
- 1/2 teaspoon paprika
- 4 carrots, cut into 1 inch pieces
- 1 head of cauliflower, cut into florets
- 1 pound of potatoes cut into 1 inch cubes
- 2 zucchinis, sliced thickly (about 1/2 inch)
- 1 bell pepper (preferably red or yellow), cut into bite size pieces
- 3 tablespoons of fresh chopped mint (use 2 if dried)

Instructions:

1. Preheat the oven to 375 degrees.
2. Clean and cut all the vegetables.
3. In a large oven-proof container that can be covered, warm the oil on the range over low to medium heat. Add the garlic and onions and sauté for 4 to 5 minutes.
4. Add the broth and the spices (ginger, pepper, and paprika), increase the heat slightly and bring to a boil.
5. Add all the vegetables and mix well. Place the covered container in the oven and cook for about 45 minutes, until the potatoes are well done (check with a fork). Stir occasionally.
6. Add the mint and serve.

Goes well with:

- Drinks: red wine.
- Other recipes: plain rice; chicken or meat recipes.

Notes/Evaluation:

Potatoes Anna (V)

Equipment needed:

potato peeler
mandoline (to thinly slice potatoes)

Special notes:

This is one of my favorite ways to eat potatoes. The recipe sounds more complicated than it really is.

Ingredients:

- 2-1/2 pounds of potatoes (either Russet or Idaho)
- 8 to 10 tablespoons butter
- 1/2 cup freshly grated Parmesan cheese
- 1 teaspoon salt
- 1 teaspoon freshly ground pepper

Instructions:

1. Scrub and peel the potatoes, and place in a bowl of cold water so they don't discolor. Slice as thin as possible (about 1/8 inch). If you have a mandoline (not the musical instrument but a slicer), it will make slicing the potatoes much easier. Keep the slices in water, but dry before using.
2. Preheat the oven to 425 degrees.
3. In a small pan melt the butter over low to medium heat.
4. In a heavy skillet pour about 1 tablespoon of the melted butter and spread around so both the bottom and the sides are well buttered.
5. Place the skillet over low heat and arrange the potato slices in a layer; drizzle with some melted butter, parmesan cheese, salt and pepper. Then build a second layer of potatoes and drizzle as above. Continue until you have used up all the potato slices.
6. When all the slices have been layered, take a dish or other round surface (e.g., the bottom of another pan), lightly oil it (you can use a cooking oil spray if you have one, or melted butter if there's any left), and use it to press down on the potato layers.
7. Cover the pan with a lid or foil and place in the oven for 30 minutes.
8. Remove the lid or foil and bake for another 30 to 35 minutes until the potatoes are crisp and brown.
9. Remove the pan from the oven and let stand for 5 minutes. Tilt the pan, using the lid or a spatula to hold the potatoes, and drain any excess butter (do this over a dish or container rather than the sink).
10. Invert the potatoes over a dish and serve, by cutting into wedges.

Goes well with:

- Drinks: depends on the main course, but likely red wine.
- Other recipes: almost any chicken recipe.

Quick Vegetable Medley

Equipment needed:

large frying pan

Special notes:

You can vary the type and proportion of vegetables, depending on what is available.

Ingredients:

- 1 tablespoon butter
- 1 medium size onion, minced
- 1/2 teaspoon cumin (a spice)
- 1 medium size bell pepper, seeded, and cut into thin strips (julienne style)
- 1 can diced green chilies (4 oz.)
- 1 butternut squash, peeled and cut into thin slices, about the thickness of a quarter
- 2 tomatoes, medium size, chopped
- 4 zucchinis, cut into thin slices, about the thickness of a quarter
- 1/2 teaspoon salt (or less)
- 1/2 teaspoon freshly ground pepper

Instructions:

1. Prepare all the ingredients.
2. Melt the butter in a large frying pan, over medium heat.
3. Add the onion and cumin and cook for 10 minutes stirring often.
4. Add the bell pepper, chilies, and butternut squash. Cook for 3 to 5 minutes stirring often.
5. Add the chopped tomatoes and zucchinis. Cover and simmer, 8 to 10 minutes, stirring occasionally.
6. Season with salt and pepper.

Goes well with:

- Drinks: red wine.
- Other recipes: most chicken recipes.

Notes/Evaluation:

Roasted Garlic Potatoes (V)

Equipment needed:

brush to clean potatoes
8 X 10-inch oven-proof baking pan

Special notes:

A very easy recipes but the results are marvelous.

Ingredients:

- 1-1/2 pounds of red potatoes
- 12 garlic cloves, unpeeled
- 3 tablespoons olive oil
- 1/2 teaspoon dried rosemary
- 1/2 teaspoon salt
- 1/2 teaspoon freshly ground pepper

Instructions:

1. Preheat the oven to 450 degrees.
2. Clean the potatoes. No need to peel them. Cut the potatoes into bite size or larger pieces. Try to have the pieces all about the same size so they all cook evenly.
3. Flatten the garlic cloves using the flat side of a knife. Place the olive oil and the flattened garlic cloves in a large-oven proof baking pan (8 X 10 or larger). Mix the potatoes well, and sprinkle the rosemary (crushing it with your fingers), salt, and pepper.
4. Roast in the oven for about 45 minutes until the potatoes are tender but crusty. Stir occasionally – about every 10 to 15 minutes. Serve hot.

Goes well with:

- Drinks: red wine.
- Other recipes: almost any meat or chicken recipe.

Notes/Evaluation:

Roasted Potatoes (V)

Equipment needed:

oven-proof baking pan

Special notes:

I have never met a person who didn't like roasted potatoes; they seem to go well with just about any main dish. This recipe is simply a slight variation from the roasted garlic potatoes recipe, with a more pronounced rosemary flavor.

Ingredients:

- 2 tablespoons olive oil
- 6 to 8 russet potatoes, cut into quarters
- 1 onion, finely chopped
- 2 teaspoons rosemary
- 2 teaspoons salt
- 1/2 teaspoon freshly ground pepper

Instructions:

1. Preheat the oven to 400 degrees.
2. Pour the olive oil in the baking pan to coat the pan. Add the potatoes, onion, and spices, and mix well.
3. Cook for 40 to 50 minutes till potatoes are golden. Turn occasionally as they cook (once or twice). Serve either directly from the baking pan or from a serving bowl.

Goes well with:

- Drinks: depends on the main course, but probably red wine.
- Other recipes: almost any chicken or meat dish.

Notes/Evaluation:

Sauteed Yellow Squash (V)

Equipment needed:

vegetable brush

Special notes:

You can substitute other vegetables for yellow squash (I like zucchinis for example), or add quartered onions, diced peppers, etc.

Ingredients:

- 1 pound yellow squash (select smaller ones)
- 1 tablespoon olive oil
- 1 teaspoon dried rosemary
- 3 tablespoons fresh lemon juice (1 or 2 lemons)
- 1/2 teaspoon salt
- 1/2 teaspoon pepper

Instructions:

1. Clean the yellow squash under cold running water; if necessary, scrub with a vegetable brush. Pat dry and slice into uniform slices the thickness of 2 nickels (about 1/8 of an inch).
2. Over medium high heat, heat the oil in a large heavy skillet. Sauté the squash for about 5 minutes, until it is golden brown but somewhat on the crunchy side.
3. Stir in the rosemary (crushing it as you do so), lemon juice, salt, and pepper. Stir and place in serving bowl.

Goes well with:

- Drinks: wine, but type depends on the main dish.
- Other recipes: goes well with any chicken or meat dish; a good accompaniment for plain risotto or most other rice dishes.

Notes/Evaluation:

Sautéed Zucchinis (V)

Equipment needed:
skillet

Special notes:
A quick recipe.

Ingredients:
- 2 tablespoons butter
- 1 tablespoon olive oil
- 1 pound zucchinis, cleaned, ends trimmed, and sliced
- 1 large onion, minced
- 4 to 6 small Roma tomatoes
- 1/2 teaspoon garlic salt
- 1/2 teaspoon freshly ground pepper
- 1/2 teaspoon oregano

Instructions:
1. Clean the zucchinis under cold water. Pat dry with a paper towel. Trim and discard the ends. Slice the thickness of a quarter.
2. In a large skillet, over medium heat, heat the butter and the olive oil. Add the zucchini slices and the minced onion and sauté for 7 to 10 minutes.
3. Add the tomatoes, the salt and pepper, and the oregano, and sauté for another 5 minutes. Serve.

Goes well with:
- Drinks: red wine like Chianti.
- Other recipes: a nice accompaniment to chicken or steaks.

Notes/Evaluation:

Simple Carrots (V)

Special notes:

This is indeed a simple, but delicious, recipe.

Ingredients:

- 2 tablespoons butter
- 2 tablespoons minced onion
- 10 carrots, peeled, cut into 2-inch segments, and each segment cut into 4 long matchsticks
- 1/2 cup beef or vegetarian broth
- 1 teaspoon brown sugar
- 1 tablespoon lemon juice (1 lemon)
- 1 tablespoon chopped fresh parsley
- 1/2 teaspoon freshly ground pepper

Instructions:

1. Melt the butter in a skillet over medium heat.
2. Add the minced onion and cook for about 2 to 3 minutes.
3. Add the carrots and stir them so they are coated with butter. Add the broth, sugar, and lemon juice, and stir.
4. Cover and let simmer for about 20 minutes, until the liquid has been absorbed.
5. Place the carrots on a serving platter, sprinkle with parsley and freshly ground pepper.

Goes well with:

- Drinks: depends on the main course as to whether red or white wine would go best.
- Other recipes: almost any chicken dish, steak, or grilled salmon steaks.

Notes/Evaluation:

Stir-fried Carrots (V)

Equipment needed:
wok
peeler

Special notes:
This is another quickie recipe. I happen to like carrots, and they go well with a variety of dishes.

Ingredients:
- 1 tablespoon vegetable oil
- 6 to 8 carrots, peeled and sliced diagonally into 1/2-inch slices
- 1/4 teaspoon salt
- 1/4 teaspoon freshly ground pepper
- 1/4 teaspoon dry thyme

Instructions:
1. Have the carrots ready in a bowl.
2. Heat the wok over medium-high heat. Add the oil, and swirl the wok so the oil is spread out.
3. Add the carrots and stir-fry for about 5 minutes.
4. Place in serving dish; sprinkle with salt, pepper, and thyme.

Goes well with:
- Drinks: beer; red wine; tea.
- Other recipes: this goes well as a side dish with almost any chicken or meat dish.

Notes/Evaluation:

Stir-fried Vegetables (V)

Equipment needed:

wok or other container for stir-frying

Special notes:

This recipe can be a meal in itself, or a side portion with a main course. For variation, you can add other vegetables, such as sliced green onions, sliced mushrooms, or broccoli flowerets.

Ingredients:

- 1 teaspoon peanut oil
- 1/2 teaspoon sesame oil
- 4 carrots sliced diagonally into small slices
- 1 red bell pepper, cut into matchstick size pieces
- 6 garlic cloves, minced
- 1/2 pound snow peas
- 1 teaspoon minced fresh ginger (or 1/2 teaspoon dry)
- 1 tablespoon soy sauce

Instructions:

1. Heat the wok over medium to medium-high heat. When it's hot, add the peanut oil and the sesame oil, and swirl so that the surface of the wok is covered with oil (about 2/3 of the way up).
2. Add the carrots and stir-fry for 3 to 4 minutes.
3. Add all the other ingredients and stir-fry until all vegetables are crisp and tender, about 3 to 5 minutes.
4. Serve.

Goes well with:

- Drinks: hot tea.
- Other recipes: can be a meal in itself (especially if you add other vegetables), or serve with rice. Goes well with many chicken or meat recipes, or even a salad.

Notes/Evaluation:

Vegetable Medley (V)

Equipment needed:

oven-proof large roasting pan (about 11 X 17 inches)

Special notes:

Here's another way to prepare a vegetable medley. Again, you can vary the type of vegetable used.

Ingredients:

- 1 teaspoon dried thyme
- 1 teaspoon dried oregano
- 1 teaspoon dried rosemary
- 1 teaspoon salt
- 1 teaspoon freshly ground pepper

- 2 tablespoons olive oil
- 6 potatoes, cut into eighths
- 1 red onion, quartered
- 1/2 teaspoon salt
- 2 bell peppers (any color), cut into chunks
- 10 to 12 carrots, cut into 2-inch pieces
- 1 head cauliflower, cut into chunks
- 1/4 lemon cut into thin slices
- 2 more tablespoons of olive oil

Instructions:

1. Preheat the oven to 425 degrees.
2. In a small clean jar (or a container with a cover) mix the thyme, oregano, rosemary, salt, and pepper.
3. In a large roasting pan (about 11 X 17 inches or larger) place the olive oil and swirl (or spread with a brush) so that the bottom and sides of the pan are oiled. Add the potatoes and onion, and sprinkle with salt. With a spoon or spatula mix the vegetables so they get coated with the oil.
4. Place in the oven and roast for 15 minutes. Meanwhile prepare the other vegetables.
5. At the end of the 15 minutes, add the other vegetables to the pan, sprinkle the mixed spices from the jar, add the lemon slices, and drizzle with the olive oil. Mix the vegetables well.
6. Return the pan to the oven and roast the vegetables for 45 minutes, mixing them with a spoon or spatula every 15 minutes.
7. When the potatoes are tender and golden brown, the medley is ready to serve. You can serve directly from the pan, or place the medley on a serving platter.

Goes well with:

- Drinks: red wine.
- Other recipes: this can be a meal in itself, or is a good accompaniment to a chicken dish.

Zucchinis Stuffed with Sausage & Provolone

Equipment needed:

frying pan
oven pan

Special notes:

Provolone is an Italian cheese; buy the imported one – it is much more flavorful than the domestic variety that can taste like a piece of rubberized plastic!

Ingredients:

- 4 zucchinis, cleaned and trimmed
- 1 teaspoon salt

- 1/4 pound Italian sausage (hot or mild; remove from casing, or buy it without the casing)
- 1/4 cup chopped onion
- 2 garlic cloves, minced

- 8 oz. fresh mushrooms, minced
- 1/4 teaspoon oregano
- 1 cup shredded Provolone

Instructions:

1. Bring a pan of water to a boil. Add a teaspoon of salt, and cook the zucchinis until they are tender (about 10 minutes); stick a fork in one of them to determine tenderness. Remove from the pan and cut in half the long way. Remove the pulp, so that you have what resembles a canoe. Set the pulp aside.

2. In a frying pan over medium heat cook the sausage, the onion, and the garlic for about 10 to 15 minutes, until the sausage meat is browned and the onion is somewhat limp. Remove mixture from skillet and set aside.

3. In the same skillet sauté the mushrooms for 3 to 5 minutes, or until tender. Add the pulp (from step 1), the sausage mixture (from step 2), and the cheese. Stir well and heat for 1 or 2 minutes.

4. Place the zucchini "canoes" in an oven-proof pan and stuff them with the mixture. Bake in a 375 degree oven for about 12 to 15 minutes, until the stuffing is heated through.

Goes well with:

- Drinks: red wine; beer.
- Other recipes: salad; chicken.

Notes/Evaluation:

VEGETABLES

Zucchini Frittata (V)

Equipment needed:

non-stick large frying pan (or one sprayed with non-stick cooking oil)
pepper grinder
colander

Special notes:

Frittata is particularly good cold, prepared a day ahead. The recipe is simple and reads more complex than it is, especially step #7.

Ingredients:

- 1 pound zucchini, thinly sliced
- 1/2 can pitted olives (black or green), thinly sliced
- 6 green onions, thinly sliced including green portion
- 1/4 teaspoon dried oregano (crush between thumb and finger to let out flavor)
- 6 eggs
- 3 tablespoons water
- 1/4 teaspoon salt
- freshly ground pepper to taste
- 2 tablespoons grated Parmesan cheese
- 4 tablespoons olive oil
- 2 garlic cloves, minced

Instructions:

1. In a big pan filled with salted (1 tablespoon) water to a height of 1/2 to 1 inch, cook the sliced zucchini for 5 minutes. Pour into colander and rinse with cold water. Let drain.

2. In a bowl, combine the zucchini, the olives, green onions, and oregano.

3. In a separate bowl, combine the eggs, water, salt, pepper, and cheese and gently mix together with a fork.

4. In a large, non-stick frying pan heat 3 tablespoons of oil and the garlic, until the garlic is golden. Use medium heat and do not burn the garlic.

5. Add the zucchini mixture to the frying pan, cook for about 2 minutes and stir. Make sure the mixture is distributed evenly in the pan.

6. Add the egg mixture and cook without stirring. When the egg mixture is set in the quarter inch nearest the outside edge of the pan, gently lift the egg mixture away from the edge, and let the uncooked egg mixture flow to the bottom of the pan (if necessary, tilt the pan slightly).

7. When most of the top of the frittata is no longer liquid, remove the frittata from the pan and flip over. A good way to do this is to place a large dish, upside down, over the frying pan and invert the frittata (be careful that none of the liquid drips on you). With the help of a spatula, or by tilting the dish, you should be able to slide the frittata back into the pan – first, however, you might want to add 1 tablespoon of olive oil to the frying pan.

8. Cook the frittata for about 3 more minutes, and remove the frittata from the pan, using the same technique as in step #7. You can serve the frittata hot, or save it in the refrigerator for the next day. When serving, cut into wedges like a pie.

Goes well with:

- Drinks: red wine.
- Other recipes: salad, French bread, assorted cheeses.

Notes/Evaluation:

Beverages

Brandy Alexander

Equipment needed:
cocktail shaker (or a large clean jar)

Special notes:
This is one of my favorite drinks.

Ingredients:
- 6 ounces Brandy
- 4 ounces Crème de Cacao liqueur
- 4 ounces heavy cream (whipping cream)

Instructions:
1. Chill whatever glasses you will use; goblets look elegant for this drink.
2. Put all the ingredients in a cocktail shaker, add ice cubes, and shake well.
3. Using a strainer to hold back the ice cubes, pour the drink into the chilled glasses and serve.

Goes well with:
- Other recipes: this is a "sweet" drink and is best served by itself, or with cookies.

Notes/Evaluation:

Bronx Cocktail

Equipment needed:
blender

Special notes:
I don't know why this is called a Bronx cocktail. I lived in New York for a number of years and never heard it mentioned there, but when I moved to Arizona, a newly acquired friend served it.

Ingredients:
- 2 ounces dry vermouth
- 2 ounces sweet vermouth
- 6 ounces gin
- 12 ounces orange juice, chilled

Instructions:
1. Chill whatever glasses you are going to use.
2. Place all the ingredients in a blender with about 8 to 10 ice cubes.
3. Whirl the ingredients for a few seconds.
4. Using a sieve to hold back any chunks of ice, pour the drink into the chilled glasses.

Goes well with:
- Other recipes: crackers with cheese; tortilla chips with salsa.

Notes/Evaluation:

Champagne Cocktail

Equipment needed:
champagne goblets

Special notes:
This is one of the easiest cocktails to prepare, yet also one of the most elegant.

Ingredients:
- 4 lumps of sugar
- Angostura bitters
- 1 bottle Brut champagne, well chilled
- 1 lemon

Instructions:
1. In each glass place a lump of sugar. Add to each lump 1 or 2 drops of Angostura.
2. Pour the champagne (tilt the glass slightly as you pour and the foam will not overflow).
3. To each glass add a one-inch piece of the lemon rind (twist before adding).
4. Enjoy!

Goes well with:
- Other recipes: an elegant drink that goes well with just about anything (except potato chips…).

Notes/Evaluation:

Champagne Punch

Equipment needed:
punch bowl

Special notes:
You can double or triple this recipe depending upon the number of guests. Make sure all your ingredients and bar ware are ice cold.

Ingredients:
- 1 orange, thinly sliced (wash but do not peel)
- 1 lemon, thinly sliced (wash but do not peel)
- 1 peach, thinly sliced (wash but do not peel)
- 1/2 cup sugar
- 6 ounces of Brandy
- 6 ounces of Benedictine liqueur (or use 12 ounces of B and B liqueur, which has Brandy and Benedictine already mixed)
- 1 bottle Brut Champagne, cold
- 8 ounces cold sparkling water or club soda (optional)
- strawberries for garnish (optional)

Instructions:
1. Either buy or make a block of ice that will fit comfortably in the punch bowl. You can use an empty quart milk container or other plastic container; rinse well, fill with water, and freeze.
2. Chill whatever glasses you will use (punch glasses are usually small, about "hand-size").
3. In the punch bowl place the orange slices, lemon slices, peach slices, sugar, and liqueurs (either the two separately or the B and B). Seal the bowl with plastic wrap and place in the freezer for about 30 to 45 minutes.
4. When ready to serve, place the block of ice in the bowl, add a bottle of cold Champagne and, if you like, about 8 ounces of cold sparkling water or club soda.
5. Stir gently and ladle the punch into the chilled glasses. Garnish each glass with a strawberry.

Goes well with:
- Other recipes: this punch can be served with almost any appetizers, with munchies, or crackers with cheese, as a prelude to brunch, lunch, or dinner.

Notes/Evaluation:

Cocoa, Coffee & Crème

Equipment needed:
saucepan

Special notes:
A festive non-alcoholic drink, excellent on a cold evening; you can also add a shot of a "coffee" liqueur like Kahlua, Bailey's cream, Amaretto, or even Irish whiskey, to make it even more festive! Real whipped cream tastes much better than the one in aerosol containers; if you don't know how to make whipped cream see step #4 for the Irish coffee recipe.

Ingredients:
- 2 cups milk
- 1 cup strong coffee (try espresso if possible)
- 1/3 cup of sugar
- 1/4 cup unsweetened cocoa
- 1 teaspoon powdered cinnamon
- 1/4 teaspoon powdered nutmeg

- whipped cream
- cinnamon for sprinkling (or cinnamon sticks to use as swizzle sticks)

Instructions:
1. In a saucepan combine the milk, coffee, sugar, cocoa, cinnamon, and nutmeg and heat over medium heat for about 5 to 10 minutes until the cocoa and sugar are dissolved, and the beverage is hot. Do not boil, and stir frequently.
2. Pour into mugs, top with whipped cream, and sprinkle with cinnamon.

Goes well with:
- Drinks: a second cup of the same!
- Other recipes: goes well as a dessert drink with cake.

Notes/Evaluation:

Frozen Blue Margaritas

Equipment needed:
margarita glasses (optional)
blender

Special notes:
Margaritas are very popular in the Southwest and can be made in countless ways, although all have tequila and lime juice as basic ingredients.

Ingredients:
- 1 lime
- 1 container margarita salt
- 12 ounces prepared Margarita mix
- 4 ounces tequila (don't use a cheap brand)
- 2 ounces of Triple Sec
- 4 ounces blue Curacao liqueur

Instructions:
1. Cut the lime into wedges. Rub the rim of each glass with a cut wedge and dip the glass into the salt. Shake off the excess salt.
2. In the blender place the Margarita mix, tequila, Triple Sec, and Curacao. Add 3 or 4 ice cubes and blend. Continue adding ice cubes 3 or 4 at a time until you have a frozen sludgy mixture.
3. Pour into glasses.

Goes well with:
- Other recipes: any munchies; tortilla chips with guacamole; crackers with cheese.

Notes/Evaluation:

Frozen Imperial Cocktail

Equipment needed:
electric blender or cocktail shaker (or a jar)

Special notes:
You can serve this drink in Champagne flutes, which makes it look even more elegant.

Ingredients:
- 4 oz. orange juice
- 3 oz. Galliano (available in most liquor stores)
- 4 teaspoons sugar
- 12 ice cubes

- dash of grenadine
- Maraschino cherries (optional)

Instructions:
1. Blend the first four ingredients.
2. Pour into glasses, add dash of grenadine and garnish with cherry.
3. Makes 2 drinks. Repeat procedure for two more.

Goes well with:
- Other recipes: munchies, like peanuts, canapés, etc.

Notes/Evaluation:

Frozen Peach Daiquiris

Equipment needed:
blender

Special notes:
A great drink on a hot summer day.

Ingredients:
- 1/2 cup rum
- 4 tablespoons lime or lemon juice (2 lemons)
- 3 tablespoons powdered sugar
- 6 ripe peaches, pitted and quartered
- ice cubes
- sprigs of mint (optional)

Instructions:
1. Place the first four items (rum through peaches) in a blender and blend well.
2. Add ice cubes 4 or 5 at a time and blend until the mixture is quite slushy.
3. Pour into margarita-type glasses (or whatever you have). If you like, decorate each glass with a sprig of mint.

Goes well with:
- Other recipes: goes well with "plain" snacks, like pretzels.

Notes/Evaluation:

Irish Coffee

Equipment needed:
4 Irish coffee glasses

electric mixer

Special notes:
When I was in graduate school and dating the young lady who eventually became my wife, one of our favorite stops was the Buena Vista Café in San Francisco's Fisherman's Wharf to have their Irish coffee. This is a great drink when the weather is cold and damp.

Ingredients:
- 1 pot of freshly brewed coffee on the strong side (use Starbucks or similar beans)
- 1 small container of heavy (whipping) cream, cold
- 4 teaspoons sugar
- 1/2 teaspoon vanilla flavoring
- sugar
- Irish whiskey

Instructions:
1. Put the mixer bowl and beaters in the freezer.
2. Brew your coffee as you usually do, but make it on the strong side. I use a good quality bean from Starbucks, and grind my own. I also use paper filters, and remove the grounds as soon as the coffee is done.
3. Fill each glass with very hot water, and let sit.
4. Prepare the whipped cream using an electric mixer and the ice cold bowl and beaters. Whip the heavy cream at medium high speed until it begins to thicken, then add the 4 teaspoons of sugar and the vanilla. Continue to beat until the cream forms solid peaks (do NOT overbeat or you will have some nice butter!).
5. When both the coffee and the cream are ready, empty the water from the glasses.
6. In each glass place in order: 1 teaspoon of sugar, two shots of Irish whiskey, and 4 ounces of coffee. Stir and add 2 tablespoons (or more) of the whipped cream (do not overfill with the cream or it will flow over the glass as it melts).
7. Serve and enjoy.

Goes well with:
- Other recipes: this is a drink to be served by itself (in front of a roaring fireplace) or at the end of a meal.

Notes/Evaluation:

Mexican Hot Chocolate

Equipment needed:

eggbeater (rotary or electric)

Special notes:

Mexican hot chocolate is a bit more flavorful than the American variety, has cinnamon in it, and is beaten until frothy.

Ingredients:

- 3 ounces unsweetened chocolate, chopped in small bits
- 4 tablespoon sugar
- 1 teaspoon cinnamon
- 1/2 teaspoon salt
- 2 teaspoons ground nutmeg

- 1 quart milk
- 1/2 cup whipping cream
- 1 teaspoon vanilla extract

Instructions:

1. In a bowl combine the first five ingredients (chocolate through nutmeg) and mix well.
2. Heat the milk and cream until it is almost boiling. Add the vanilla extract, and pour the milk over the dry ingredients, stirring well with the egg beater. When the mixture is frothy, pour into mugs and serve.

Goes well with:

- Other recipes: serve with cookies, particularly hard ones like biscottis.

Notes/Evaluation:

BEVERAGES

Peach Smoothee

Equipment needed:
electric blender

Special notes:
A nonalcoholic drink that can be enjoyed by both children and adults.

Ingredients:
- 4 peaches
- 4 cups of milk
- 2 cups vanilla ice cream
- 8 ice cubes

Instructions:
1. Wash the peaches well under cold water. Slice them into quarters and remove the pit (if you want, you can remove the skin also).
2. Place all the ingredients in the blender and blend well.
3. Serve in tall glasses. If you want to, you can garnish each glass with a slice of orange, a cherry, a strawberry, or even a little paper parasol.

Goes well with:
- Other recipes: you can serve this drink by itself especially on a summer day, or as a prelude to a meal.

Notes/Evaluation:

Ramos Gin Fizz

Equipment needed:
cocktail shaker (or a large clean jar)

Special notes:
I've had this drink in both San Francisco and in New Orleans; in both places it is popularly served at Sunday brunches. Please note that some people might object to this recipe because it uses raw egg whites.

Ingredients:
- 4 tablespoons lemon juice (2 lemons)
- 4 teaspoons powdered sugar
- 4 egg whites
- 4 tablespoons heavy cream
- 4 ounces Triple Sec liqueur
- 12 ounces gin
- 1 bottle club soda

Instructions:
1. Chill the glasses you will use (tall water glasses are fine), and the club soda.
2. Place the first six ingredients (everything but the club soda) in a cocktail shaker (or large jar), add about 10 to 12 ice cubes and shake well.
3. Using a strainer to hold back the ice cubes, pour the drink into the four chilled glasses. To each glass add some ice cold club soda (about 2 shots each) and stir.

Goes well with:
- Other recipes: a good drink to serve at a brunch, with a variety of other foods or appetizers.

Notes/Evaluation:

BEVERAGES

Salty Dog

Equipment needed:
ice cube grinder to make shaved ice (optional)

cocktail shaker (or large clean jar)

Special notes:
This is a refreshing drink with a punch.

Ingredients:
- 12 ounces grapefruit juice
- 12 ounces gin
- 1/2 teaspoon salt
- shaved ice (optional)
- celery stalks (optional)

Instructions:
1. Chill whatever glasses you will use (highball-type glasses are fine).
2. Place the first 3 ingredients in a cocktail shaker (or large jar), add ice cubes and shake well.
3. Fill each glass half full with shaved ice (or ice cubes), and pour the drink over the ice.
4. If you wish, decorate each glass with a stirrer made from a short celery stalk (leave the green leaves).

Goes well with:
- Other recipes: almost any munchies; tortilla chips with salsa; crackers with cheese; pretzels, etc.

Notes/Evaluation:

Sangria (Red Wine Punch)

Special notes:

If this sangria is too hearty, you can add some iced sparkling water or club soda to dilute the wine flavor.

Ingredients:

- 1 bottle (750 ml) red wine, like Burgundy
- 1/2 cup sugar
- 1 lemon, washed and sliced
- 1 orange, washed and sliced
- 12 strawberries, washed

Instructions:

1. Pour the wine into a large pitcher. Add the sugar and mix well.
2. Add the fruit, and let the pitcher sit in the refrigerator for several hours (or overnight).
3. Serve into glasses.

Goes well with:

- Other recipes: a good brunch drink, goes well with a variety of appetizers.

Notes/Evaluation:

Desserts

Baked Pears with Yogurt Sauce (V)

Equipment needed:
oven-proof container (like a Pyrex glass pan)

Special notes:
An easy but elegant dessert. Don't cut the pears too early or they might get brown.

Ingredients:
- 4 pears (Bartlett or Bosc), halved and cored
- 4 tablespoons of Amaretto (almond-flavored liqueur)
- 2 egg yolks
- 1/2 cup natural (or unflavored) yogurt
- 1/4 teaspoon cardamon (a spice)
- 1/4 teaspoon nutmeg (another spice)
- 2 tablespoons honey
- 1 tablespoon lemon juice
- 2 tablespoons brandy

Instructions:
1. Take each half of a pear and remove a small slice from the curved uncut half, so the pear will sit rather than wobble. Place the pear halves in an ovenproof container, and sprinkle the Amaretto over them.
2. Bake in 350 degree oven for about 45 minutes, until the pears are tender (test one by piercing with a fork or toothpick).
3. Meantime, blend all the other ingredients in a pan and cook over low medium heat until the mixture begins to thicken, about 15 minutes,
4. Place the pears in serving dishes and spoon the hot sauce over them.

Goes well with:
- Drinks: coffee.
- Other recipes: a good dessert following just about any main dish, like a chicken recipe.

Notes/Evaluation:

Bananas Foster (V)

Equipment needed:

chafing dish

Special notes:

This dessert originated in New Orleans and is an elegant, flamed dessert prepared at the table, and served in a number of elegant restaurants. If you do prepare it at the table, you will need a heat source – either a chafing dish, or an electric skillet, or in step #3 you can bring the pan to the table and ignite the rum there.

Ingredients:

- 4 firm but ripe bananas
- 2 tablespoons butter (at room temperature)
- 4 teaspoons brown sugar
- 1/4 teaspoon ground cinnamon
- 1/8 teaspoon ground nutmeg
- vanilla ice cream
- 2 ounces rum

Notes/Evaluation:

Instructions:

1. In the chafing dish mix the butter and sugar. Cook over medium heat for about 3 minutes. Peel the bananas, slice them in half lengthwise, and then slice each half into 3 or 4 pieces. Add the bananas to the chafing dish and stir, so the bananas become coated with the butter and sugar – about 5 minutes or so. Sprinkle with cinnamon and nutmeg. (If you use a pan rather than a chafing dish, do the same thing over medium heat).

2. At this point spoon some vanilla ice cream into individual bowls, one for each person.

3. Add the rum to the chafing dish and wait about a minute for the rum to get warm. Using a long wooden match (the fireplace type), flame the rum.

4. Spoon the bananas, sauce, and flaming rum into each of the ice cream bowls.

5. Serve.

Goes well with:

- Drinks: coffee.
- Other recipes: a great finish for almost any main course; you might want to serve some cookies, especially light, flaky ones.

Capirotada (Bread Pudding) (V)

Equipment needed:

oven-proof baking dish, about 2-quart size, as well as another one slightly larger

Special notes:

This recipe calls for croissants, but you could use any of a wide variety of breads, like French or even (gulp) American bread. You can also add a variety of ingredients to this dessert, like cheese or sliced apples. This recipe calls for a cooking technique called "bagno Maria," or in English "water bath" (note how the Italians intertwine cooking and sex…).

Ingredients:

- 1 butter stick
- 6 fresh croissants
- 1 cup seedless raisins
- 6 eggs
- 1/2 cup brown sugar
- 1/2 cup sherry
- 1 teaspoon vanilla
- 1/2 teaspoon ground cinnamon
- 1/2 teaspoon grated nutmeg
- 3 cups milk

Instructions:

1. Using the stick of butter, butter well the bottom and sides of a 2-quart baking dish.
2. Cut the croissants into 1/2-inch cubes. Spread the cubes in the buttered pan.
3. Sprinkle the raisins over the croissant cubes.
4. In a separate bowl whisk together the eggs, sugar, sherry, vanilla extract, cinnamon, and nutmeg. Whisk in the milk.
5. Pour the mixture over the croissant cubes and let stand for about 30 minutes.
6. Preheat the oven to 375 degrees.
7. Now comes the tricky part. You will need to bake the pudding in a water bath or "bagno Maria," as the Italians say. To do this you need to place the 2-quart baking dish into a larger container filled with hot water, and have both in the oven. The easiest way to do this is to place both containers in the oven and THEN pour the hot water into the larger container (I have an electric tea kettle that is just about right for this purpose).
8. Bake the pudding for about an hour. To test readiness, insert a knife in the center; if the pudding is ready, the blade should be clean when you remove it.
9. Spoon the pudding into individual dishes or bowls. Some people like the pudding with a dollop of whipped cream or ice cream.

Goes well with:

- Drinks: coffee or tea.
- Other recipes: a good dessert for practically any meal.

Cherries Jubilee (V)

Equipment needed:

chafing dish or electric skillet

Special notes:

This is a very festive and elegant dessert served in many continental restaurants, and prepared at the table. It is one of the easiest desserts to prepare. You can cut the recipe in half for a very romantic finale to a dinner for two.

Ingredients:

- vanilla ice cream
- 2 cans of pitted cherries
- 4 tablespoons freshly squeezed lemon juice (1 or 2 lemons)
- 3/4 cup of sugar
- 1/2 cup brandy

Instructions:

1. Place 2 scoops of vanilla ice cream in each of 4 containers (ice cream dishes if you have them, or dessert bowls). Place the dishes with the ice cream in your freezer till you are ready.
2. Drain the cherries well. Strain the lemon juice to remove the seeds.
3. To prepare at table-side, you will need a chafing dish (or an electric skillet) and all the ingredients ready. Light the chafing dish.
4. In the chafing dish place the cherries, sugar, and lemon juice. Combine well with a spoon and bring to a boil.
5. Add the brandy, wait a few seconds, and light with a long-handled wooden match. The mixture should flame.
6. Spoon the flaming mixture over each ice cream portion and serve.

Goes well with:

- Drinks: coffee, especially a cappuccino.
- Other recipes: an elegant ending to a fine meal, especially a meat dish.

Notes/Evaluation:

Chocolate Biscotti (V)

Equipment needed:

cookie sheet
wire racks for cooling
cheese grater
spatula

Special notes:

Biscotto is really a generic Italian word for cookie, but it also means a particular type of cookie that has been baked twice. I knew biscotti as a child in Italy, and was pleasantly surprised when some years ago they became popular in the United States.

Ingredients:

- vegetable shortening (comes in a big can labeled "Crisco")
- 1 stick of butter, softened
- 1 cup sugar
- 2 eggs
- 1 teaspoon finely grated orange peel
- 1 teaspoon finely grated lemon peel
- 1/4 cup slivered almonds

- 3-1/2 cups all purpose flour
- 1 teaspoon baking powder
- 1/2 teaspoon salt
- 1 cup cocoa in powdered form

Instructions:

1. Preheat the oven to 350 degrees.
2. Lightly grease a cookie sheet by using a small piece of wax paper as a "brush" – dip into the can of vegetable shortening ("Crisco"), and spread the shortening over the entire bottom surface.
3. In a large bowl mix well the butter, sugar, eggs, grated orange peel, grated lemon peel, and almonds.
4. In a separate bowl whisk the flour, baking powder, salt, and cocoa.
5. A little at a time, stir the flour mixture into the butter-sugar-egg mixture, until the two mixtures are well blended.
6. Separate the mixture into two equal portions and shape each into a flattened half log about 10 inches long and 3 inches wide. You can do this by wrapping the dough in plastic wrap and rolling it into shape. If you use your bare hands, lightly flour them to prevent the dough from sticking.
7. Bake on the cookie sheet for 30 minutes, then remove from oven and cool on a rack for about 15 minutes until you can handle the logs without personal injury. Do NOT shut the oven off.

8. Slice each log into 1/2-inch slices as uniform as possible. Place the slices cut side down on the cookie sheet. Put back in the oven and bake for 10 minutes; then with a spatula flip each biscotto over and cook for another 8 to 10 minutes.
9. Remove from oven and place the individual biscotti on a wire rack to cool.
10. Store in airtight container.

Goes well with:

- Drinks: coffee; hot chocolate; hot herbal tea.
- Other recipes: goes well at the end of any meal, with a hot beverage.

Notes/Evaluation:

Crème Brulee (Caramel Custard) (V)

Equipment needed:

small individual ramekins or small bowls
a double boiler (two pans, one fits inside the other – hot water goes into the lower pan and the ingredients in the top pan)
a wooden spoon

Special notes:

You will find this dessert listed in many restaurant menus; it is actually quite easy to make and worth the effort.

Ingredients:

- 4 cups heavy (whipping) cream (1 quart container)
- 8 egg yolks
- 1/2 cup sugar
- 1 teaspoon vanilla extract
- 1/2 cup light brown sugar
- 6 to 8 strawberries for decoration (optional)

Instructions:

1. In a small pan heat the heavy cream over medium low heat, just until bubbles begin to appear.
2. Meanwhile, in a double boiler over hot water and using medium to medium-low heat, whisk the egg yolks, and blend in the sugar a tablespoon at a time. When the heavy cream is ready (step 1), stir the cream into the egg-sugar mixture, a bit at a time, stirring with a wooden spoon. Cook for approximately 15 minutes until it is thickened. Stir in the vanilla.
3. Pour the custard into individual ramekins or bowls, cover with plastic wrap and refrigerate overnight.
4. When you are almost ready to serve the crème brulee, preheat the broiler for about 10 to 15 minutes. Place the filled cups (without the plastic wrap) on a baking sheet or other flat surface, then sprinkle each with light brown sugar and place under the broiler, about 2 or 3 inches below the heating element. Let the brown sugar melt and slightly "burn." Remove from broiler.
5. You can serve this custard hot, or refrigerate for about 1 hour. If you want, you can decorate each with a strawberry.

Goes well with:

- Drinks: coffee, hot tea.
- Other recipes: an elegant dessert that both compliments and complements any meal.

Notes/Evaluation:

Formaggio Crema (Cream Cheese Dessert) (V)

Equipment needed:

4 stemmed glasses
electric beaters

Special notes:

This recipe called for "mascarpone," an Italian cheese that can be difficult to obtain in the United States, and expensive when available. Cream cheese will do just as well.

Ingredients:

- 1 package cream cheese (8 ounces)
- 1/2 cup powdered (confectioner's) sugar
- 1/4 cup heavy (whipping) cream
- 1 egg yolk
- 4 tablespoons brandy
- decoration (see step #3)

Instructions:

1. In a bowl beat (using electric beaters) the cream cheese, sugar, cream, and egg yolk, until the mixture has a light consistency (like pudding). Stir in the brandy.
2. Spoon the mixture into four stemmed glasses and chill for two or more hours.
3. Before serving, decorate with a sprig of mint, or some chocolate shavings, or some non-pareil (those tiny colored spheres), or even maraschino cherries.

Goes well with:

- Other recipes: cookies; a great finish to any Italian recipe.

Notes/Evaluation:

Peach Cobbler (V)

Equipment needed:
glass baking pan (11 X 7 inches or similar size)
mixer

Special notes:
A cobbler is essentially a fruit pie with a crust that is either at the bottom or at the top. You can use a wide variety of fruit, either in combination or all of one kind.

Ingredients:
- 6 ripe peaches
- 2 cups sugar
- 1 cup all purpose flower
- 1 teaspoon baking soda
- 1/4 teaspoon salt
- 1/2 teaspoon cinnamon
- 1 cup milk
- 1/2 teaspoon vanilla extract
- 4 tablespoons butter, softened
- vanilla ice cream or whipped cream (optional)

Instructions:
1. Preheat the oven to 350 degrees.
2. Wash the peaches, dry, and slice as evenly as possible (about 12 to 16 slices per peach).
3. Distribute the slices evenly in an 11 X 7 glass baking pan. Sprinkle 1 cup of sugar over the peaches.
4. In a mixer bowl blend together the remaining ingredients – 1 cup sugar, flour, baking soda, salt, cinnamon, milk, vanilla extract, and 4 tablespoons of butter.
5. Spoon the batter over the peach slices.
6. Bake for approximately 45 minutes until the batter is golden brown.
7. Remove from oven and let cool for 15 to 20 minutes.
8. Serve topped with vanilla ice cream or whipped cream.

Goes well with:
- Drinks: coffee, tea, or milk.
- Other recipes: almost any main course.

Notes/Evaluation:

Rice Pudding (V)

Equipment needed:
cheese grater

Special notes:
Another easy-to-make dessert.

Ingredients:
- 1/2 cup dark raisins
- 1/3 cup rum
- 2 tablespoons sugar
- 2 tablespoons cinnamon
- 3/4 cup white rice (not instant)
- 3 cups milk
- 1/2 grated orange rind (1 orange)
- whipped cream (optional; you can make your own – see recipe for Irish coffee – or use a commercial product)

Instructions:
1. In a small bowl place the raisins and the rum and let them soak.
2. In a small jar combine 2 tablespoons of sugar and 2 tablespoons of cinnamon and shake well to mix.
3. In a saucepan over medium-high heat, combine the rice, milk, and cinnamon-sugar, and bring to a simmer. Add the grated orange rind, reduce the heat, cover the saucepan, and simmer for about 15 to 20 minutes until the rice is tender.
4. Add the raisin and rum mixture and mix well, cooking for a few more minutes.
5. Place the pudding in a bowl, cover the surface with plastic wrap and let chill in refrigerator.
6. You can serve the pudding at room temperature or cold. For an extra touch, serve with whipped cream.

Goes well with:
- Drinks: coffee, tea, or milk.
- Other recipes: almost any main dish (but not a rice dish).

Notes/Evaluation:

Stuffed Peaches (V)

Equipment needed:
baking dish

Special notes:
A simple but elegant dessert.

Ingredients:
- 1 can cling peach halves (or 4 large fresh peaches)
- 2 tablespoons butter, softened at room temperature
- 2 tablespoons sugar
- 3/4 cup cookie crumbs (use your favorite cookie – macaroons or hazelnut cookies are often used)
- 1 egg yolk, beaten
- 2 tablespoons cognac or brandy
- 4 tablespoons Marsala or sweet sherry
- 1/4 cup peach juice from the can (or water if you use fresh peaches)

Instructions:
1. Using a fork, blend the butter and sugar well, in a bowl.
2. Add the cookie crumbs, egg yolk, and cognac, and mix well.
3. Place the peaches in a buttered baking dish. In the center of each peach half, place a dollop of the cookie mixture (if the peach halves don't sit right, shave off a tiny slice from the uncut part to give each a flat base). Sprinkle the Marsala on top. Pour the peach juice (or water) into the baking dish.
4. Bake for 15 to 20 minutes (25 to 30 for fresh peaches), in a 350 degree oven.

Goes well with:
- Drinks: a little sip of Marsala or sherry.
- Other recipes: a nice dessert for any meal, especially with chicken as the main course.

Notes/Evaluation:

Vanilla Ice Cream with Rum Sauce (V)

Equipment needed:

cheese grater
juice extractor (optional)
small sieve
pastry brush

Special notes:

You can turn ordinary ice cream into a very special dessert simply by the topping. Here is a relatively easy example.

Ingredients:

- 1/2 gallon vanilla ice cream
- 3 oranges, washed
- 1/2 cup orange juice (either from the oranges or separate)
- 2 tablespoons butter
- 4 tablespoons sugar
- 1/3 cup dark rum

Instructions:

1. Wash and dry the oranges. Using a cheese grater over a piece of wax paper, grate the rind of the oranges, and set aside.
2. If you use already squeezed orange juice, skip this step. Otherwise, have a small bowl with a sieve over it. Roll the oranges over a flat surface, cut in half, and squeeze the juice into the sieve so the seeds will be caught. If you have one, you can use a glass juicer to extract the juice, or you can spear the orange half with a fork to hold more easily and extract the juice by hand.
3. In a small pan place the orange juice and butter, and over moderate heat let it come to a boil. If necessary, decrease the heat and let it simmer for about 10 to 15 minutes until the liquid is reduced by half.
4. Add the sugar and grated orange rind and stir. With a brush dipped in cold water, wash down any sugar crystals that might cling to the sides of the pan. Continue to simmer and stir until the sugar is dissolved.
5. Add the rum, stir, and spoon the sauce over individual dishes of ice cream.

Goes well with:

- Drinks: coffee, tea, or milk.
- Other recipes: cookies; a good dessert for almost any meal.

Notes/Evaluation:

DESSERTS

Valerie's Cheesecake with Peaches (V)

Equipment needed:

10-inch glass pie pan
mixer

Special notes:

My wife, Valerie, is a fantastic cook. This is one of her recipes, and one of my favorites.

Ingredients:

- butter or vegetable shortening
- 3/4 cup all purpose flour
- 1 teaspoon baking powder
- 1/2 teaspoon salt
- 1 package (3-1/4 ounces) vanilla pudding mix (not instant)
- 3 tablespoons butter, softened
- 1/2 cup milk
- 1 egg
- 1 can (15 ounces) sliced peaches
- 1 package (8 ounces) cream cheese, softened
- 1/2 cup sugar
- 3 tablespoons peach juice (from the above can)
- 1 tablespoon sugar mixed with 1/2 teaspoon cinnamon

Instructions:

1. Preheat the oven to 325 degrees.
2. Grease well the bottom and sides of a 10-inch glass pie pan (use a piece of wax paper as a brush – you can use butter or vegetable shortening).
3. In a mixer bowl combine the flour, baking powder, vanilla pudding mix, butter, milk, and one egg, and beat at a medium speed for 2 minutes. Pour the mixture into the pan.
4. Drain the peaches well, but save the liquid.
5. Arrange the peach slices over the batter in a concentric or similar pattern.
6. In a small mixer bowl combine the cream cheese, sugar, and 3 tablespoons of peach juice, and beat at medium speed for 2 minutes. Spoon over the peaches (but NOT the outer 1-inch periphery).
7. In a small empty jar mix the 1 tablespoon of sugar with the cinnamon well, and sprinkle the cinnamon sugar over the pie.
8. Bake in the oven for 30 to 35 minutes until the crust is golden brown.
9. Cool and the place in refrigerator.
10. Serve cold. This can be made a day ahead.

Goes well with:

- Drinks: milk, coffee, or tea.
- Other recipes: goes well with just about any main dish.

White Chocolate Ice Cream

Equipment needed:

ice cream maker
whisk (optional, you can use a fork)

Special notes:

Once you've tasted homemade ice cream, you will never go back to commercial products. If you're counting calories, this is probably not for you! If you can, buy white chocolate from a chocolate shop.

Ingredients:

- 2 cups half and half
- 2 cups whipping cream
- 1/2 cup sugar
- 6 egg yolks
- 8 ounces white chocolate, chopped into bits

Instructions:

1. Use a heavy medium saucepan. Pour the half and half, whipping cream, and sugar in it and stir over medium heat.
2. In a large bowl whisk the eggs, then whisk the hot milk mixture into the eggs. When all is blended well, pour everything back into the saucepan, continue heating over medium heat, and stir until the mixture thickens. Add the chocolate a bit at a time so it melts. Don't let the mixture boil – if necessary, reduce the heat and/or lift the pan away from the heating element.
3. When all the chocolate has melted, pour the mixture back into the bowl, cover with plastic wrap and refrigerate until cold.
4. To make the ice cream, follow the instructions that came with your ice cream maker.

Goes well with:

- Other recipes: almost any meal is complemented by ice cream.

Notes/Evaluation:

White and Green Ice Cream Pie (V)

Equipment needed:

food processor (or bowl)
10-inch pie pan

Special notes:

Ice cream pies are very easy to make, especially if you buy both the pie crust and the ice cream! You can use any type of ice cream or frozen yogurt, and you can add all sorts of ingredients, such as chopped up candy bars, peanut butter, fresh fruit like blueberries, toasted nuts, orange and/or lemon juice, and so on.

Ingredients:

- stick of butter
- 2 packages chocolate wafers
- 1/4 cup of sugar
- (or a commercially made pie crust for a 10-inch pie)
- 2 quarts vanilla ice cream
- 4 shots crème de menthe

Instructions:

1. If you use a commercially prepared pie crust, skip to step #8. Otherwise, preheat the oven to 350 degrees.
2. Lightly rub a stick of butter over the bottom and sides of your pie pan.
3. Place the wafers in a sturdy plastic bag, and using the bottom of a jar or a rolling pin, crumble the wafers to very fine crumbs. You should end up with 1-1/2 cups of crumbs.
4. In a small saucepan over low heat, melt 6 tablespoons of the butter.
5. In your food processor (or in a bowl), place the crumbs, sugar, and butter. Mix together with a fork (or with the processor).
6. Spoon the mixture into the pie pan and spread evenly on the bottom and on the sides. You can use the flat bottom of a jar or drinking glass to press down on the crumbs and make the surface even.
7. Bake the crust in the oven for about 10 to 15 minutes until it is firm to the touch. Let it cool to room temperature, and then place in the freezer for about 2 hours.
8. Leave the ice cream container in the refrigerator rather than the freezer, so the ice cream becomes slightly soft and more easily handled; this should take about 30 minutes.

9. Fill the pie crust about halfway with the ice cream. With a narrow spatula pack the ice cream well. Sprinkle two shots of the crème de menthe over the surface. Continue packing the ice cream. Sprinkle two more shots of crème de menthe on the surface. Cover with plastic wrap and place in the freezer for a minimum of two hours.

10. About 1/2 hour before serving, place pie in the refrigerator. Slicing the pie can be a bit challenging. It helps if you dip the knife in hot water and dry it before you use it.

Goes well with:

- Drinks: coffee, tea, hot chocolate, milk.
- Other recipes: a nice ending for any meal, particularly in the summer.

Notes/Evaluation:

Zabaglione al Rum (V)

Equipment needed:

double boiler (if you don't have one, you can use two pans, one smaller that will fit into the larger one, with the larger one having some boiling water)
Electric egg beater

Special notes:

Zabaglione is an Italian dessert that is essentially an egg custard. It is often made with Marsala, a sherry-like wine. When I was a child, my mother fed me zabaglione for breakfast, since many Italians believe that zabaglione is like chicken soup – a curative for all sorts of ills! There are many variations of the basic recipe; usually zabaglione is served hot, but this recipe is for cold zabaglione.

Ingredients:

- 4 egg yolks, at room temperature
- 2 tablespoons of sugar
- 1/4 cup dark rum
- 1/2 cup whipping cream

Instructions:

1. Whip the whipping cream, using an electric beater, till the cream makes soft peaks when you pull the beater out. Use a bowl and beaters that have been refrigerated. Set aside.
2. Place some water in the bottom of the double boiler and heat over medium heat. You will be putting the top of the double boiler into the bottom, so make sure you don't have so much water that it overflows (you might want to try a dry run...before you heat the water).
3. When the water is boiling, place the yolks and sugar into the top pan, place the top into the bottom pan, and whisk until the sugar dissolves (if you don't have a whisk, you can use a fork).
4. Add the rum and whisk until the mixture thickens and has the consistency of pudding.
5. Remove from heat and cool in a bowl of ice cubes and water.
6. When cool, gently fold in the whipped cream. Serve in mugs, dessert glasses, or bowls.

Goes well with:

- Drinks: a "creamy" wine like dessert sherry.
- Other recipes: cookies.

Notes/Evaluation:

Bread & Breakfast

Apple Pancakes (V)

Equipment needed:

oven-proof container

Special notes:

Pancakes are very easy to make and quite versatile. You can vary the fruit (try bananas instead of apples – they're quite good), or add minced nuts like walnuts. You can top with whipped cream or jam, instead of the traditional pancake syrup. Ordinarily, pancakes are round, but in this recipe they will be pan size, and will need to be cut into individual servings.

Ingredients:

- 3 tablespoons butter
- 2 cups apple slices, thin (about 3 apples)
- 1/2 cup sugar
- 1 tablespoon ground cinnamon
- 2 cups pancake baking mix
- 1 cup skim milk
- 2 eggs

Instructions:

1. Preheat the oven to 400 degrees.
2. In an ovenproof skillet melt the butter over medium heat. (If you don't have an ovenproof skillet, use whatever skillet you have, and then in step #5 pour the mixture into an ovenproof container). Add the apple slices and stir. Cook for 2 to 3 minutes.
3. In an empty jar place the sugar and cinnamon and shake well. Sprinkle the mixture over the apples.
4. In a bowl mix the pancake mix with the skim milk and eggs.
5. Pour the mixture over the apples and bake in the oven for about 15 minutes until it is golden.
6. Invert on a serving platter and serve by cutting into individual portions.

Goes well with:

- Drinks: hot coffee, hot chocolate, or tea.
- Other recipes: a side order of bacon or sausage.

Notes/Evaluation:

Dutch Baby (V)

Equipment needed:
whisk (optional – you can use a fork)
3-quart oven-proof container (about 13 X 9 inches)

Special notes:
I don't know why this is called a Dutch baby, but it is a wonderful pancake-like concoction.

Ingredients:
- 4 eggs, at room temperature
- 1 cup milk
- 1 cup all purpose flour
- 1/3 cup of sugar
- 1/2 stick unsalted butter

- 1 jar apple sauce
- powdered sugar or your favorite fruit preserve

Instructions:
1. Preheat the oven to 425 degrees.
2. In a bowl whisk together the eggs, milk, flour, and sugar.
3. In a small pan over medium-low heat melt the butter.
4. Pour the melted butter into an oven-proof container, and make sure the butter coats all sides. Pour the egg-milk mixture into this container and bake in the oven for about 15 minutes, until it is golden and puffed up.
5. Serve immediately (it will deflate quite rapidly) with powdered sugar and apple sauce, or with a fruit preserve.

Goes well with:
- Drinks: hot coffee, hot chocolate.
- Other recipes: side order of sausage or bacon.

Notes/Evaluation:

Eggs Benedict

Equipment needed:

double boiler (two pans that fit together – bottom one has boiling water, top one has ingredients to be cooked)

whisk (optional – you can use a fork)

Special notes:

This is probably the "trickiest" recipe in this book. It is a brunch favorite; you can use ham or Canadian bacon.

Ingredients:

For the Hollandaise sauce:

- 2 tablespoons sweet butter, at room temperature
- 3 large egg yolks
- 2 tablespoons fresh lemon juice (1 lemon)
- pinch of cayenne pepper (or Tabasco sauce)
- 1/2 teaspoon salt
- 1/2 teaspoon white ground pepper

- 8 eggs
- 2 tablespoons vinegar (any kind)
- 4 English muffins, split in half
- 8 slices of ham, cut to fit the muffin halves

Instructions:

1. Make the Hollandaise sauce. You will need a double boiler (two pans, the top one fitting partway in the bottom one). Fill the bottom one with some water (not so much that it overflows when you put the top pan in – you might try this at the sink first). Over medium heat, heat the water to simmer (not boiling).

2. In the top of the double boiler place 1 tablespoon butter and let it melt. Add the egg yolks and whisk the egg mixture. Add the second tablespoon of butter and continue whisking until the ingredients are well mixed.

3. Add the lemon juice, cayenne pepper (or Tabasco), salt, and pepper, and whisk until the sauce is thickened. If it is getting too thick, lift the top pan away from the heat and/or add a few drops of warm water to the sauce. Keep the sauce warm (over low heat) while you prepare the rest.

4. Poach the eggs (this is the tricky part!). Using a large pan or skillet, fill it with about 2 or 3 inches of cold water, add 2 tablespoons of vinegar, and heat over medium heat until the water simmers. Taking one egg at a time, break the egg into a coffee cup and gently slide the egg out into the simmering water. Do this to each egg in turn, and let each egg poach (cook) in the water for about 4

minutes. Since most likely your pan won't hold all 8 eggs at one time, transfer the poached eggs to a shallow bowl of warm water (a bit on the hot side but not boiling) while you continue poaching. Incidentally, at a gourmet shop or online you might find egg poachers, little miniature stands that are placed directly in the water.

5. On a skillet warm the pieces of ham.
6. Toast the English muffin halves.
7. Now assemble the eggs Benedict: on each muffin half place the ham, then the poached egg (carefully with a spatula), and then the Hollandaise sauce.
8. Serve and enjoy!

Goes well with:

- Drinks: orange juice; coffee.
- Other recipes: side order of sausage, hash browns, bacon, etc.

Notes/Evaluation:

Focaccia (V)

Equipment needed:

brush for olive oil
cooling racks
rolling pin (optional)

Special notes:

Many Italian restaurants now serve a bread called focaccia, often with flavored oil to dip it in. You can make the dough from scratch or, as in this recipe, use already made pizza or bread dough (you can buy it frozen in a supermarket, or fresh in some bakeries). The traditional Italian focaccia is oily, with rosemary, and sometimes large grains of salt. You can however add a variety of ingredients, just as in a pizza – like garlic, olives, mushrooms, oregano, basil, or thyme.

Ingredients:

- 1 pound bread or pizza dough (if frozen, let thaw)
- Olive oil
- 1/2 cup grated Parmesan cheese
- 1 teaspoon dried rosemary

Instructions:

1. If necessary, flatten the dough to 1/2-inch thickness (use a rolling pin if you have one, otherwise an empty wine bottle will do). Shape the dough to fit whatever size pans you will use.
2. Brush the pans well with the olive oil. Put the dough in the pans, cover with plastic wrap or a clean dish towel and place on a warm surface – like near a window if it's sunny; if not, your oven at its lowest temperature will do. Let the dough rise for about 1-1/2 hours.
3. Preheat the oven to 400 degrees.
4. Using your fingers dimple the dough and drizzle with olive oil. Original focaccia is quite oily, so don't be stingy. Sprinkle with parmesan cheese and rosemary (crush the rosemary between your fingers to increase the aroma).
5. Bake the focaccia for about 25 to 30 minutes, until it is golden.
6. Remove from the oven and place pans on a cooling rack (any kind of rack set on a nonburning surface that will let the heat dissipate – you can even use a cold barbecue grill).
7. When the focaccia is warm or at room temperature, remove from the pan (gently invert the pan or use a spatula) and serve. Have some good olive oil and salt for dipping.

Goes well with:

- Drinks: red wine.
- Other recipes: focaccia can be used as a bread with almost any main dish, or goes quite well with a salad.

French Toast (V)

Equipment needed:
whisk (optional, you can use a fork)

Special notes:
One of my favorite breakfast foods. You can use a variety of breads. You can also soak the bread (step #2) overnight.

Ingredients:
- 4 eggs
- 1/3 cup of milk
- 1/3 cup orange juice
- 1/2 teaspoon vanilla
- 2 tablespoons sugar
- 1/4 teaspoon salt

- 8 slices French bread
- 3 or 4 tablespoons butter
- 4 tablespoons powdered sugar
- butter
- maple syrup

Instructions:
1. In a large bowl whisk the eggs. Add the other ingredients (milk through salt) and mix well.
2. Soak the slices of bread (one or two at a time) in the egg mixture, turning the bread until it is well coated.
3. In a skillet or griddle heat the butter over medium heat; add the slices of bread and cook until they are golden on the bottom; turn over so that both sides are golden (about 5 to 8 minutes on each side).
4. Dust each slice with powdered sugar and serve (on a platter or individual dishes). Let each person add butter and maple syrup.

Goes well with:
- Drinks: orange juice; coffee or hot tea.
- Other recipes: serve with a side order of breakfast sausage, Canadian bacon, or ham (just heat with a little bit of butter).

Notes/Evaluation:

Huevos Rancheros (Ranch-style Eggs) (V)

Equipment needed:

tongs (optional)
aluminum foil

Special notes:

Essentially these are sunny side-up eggs served on a tortilla with salsa.

Ingredients:

- 3 large tomatoes, cored and chopped well
- 4 tablespoons vegetable oil
- 1/2 onion, chopped well
- 1 clove of garlic, minced
- 1 can chopped green chilies (4 ounces)
- 1 tablespoon lemon juice (1 lemon)
- 1 tablespoon minced fresh cilantro
- 4 corn tortillas (medium size – 6 inches diameter)
- 4 eggs (for heartier appetites use 8 eggs)
- 1 fresh avocado (optional)
- 1 lime (optional)
- 1 can refried beans (optional)
- 1/2 cup shredded cheddar

Instructions:

1. First make the salsa. Clean, core, and chop the tomatoes. In a medium size skillet heat 2 tablespoons vegetable oil over medium heat. Sauté the onion and garlic till tender.

2. To the skillet add the tomatoes, chilies, lemon juice, and cilantro, and simmer.

3. If you're going to serve refried beans, now is the time to open the can, place the beans in a pan and heat over medium heat. If you like, you can add a handful (about 1/2 cup) of shredded cheddar cheese, and mix it in with the beans as they heat up. Do stir occasionally. Make sure the beans do not get burned – if necessary lower the heat.

4. In a large skillet, heat 2 tablespoons vegetable oil over medium-high heat. When the oil is hot, add the corn tortillas one at a time and fry them for about 5 seconds on each side (use tongs to turn them over). As each tortilla is done set it on paper towels so the oil drains, and then wrap them in foil to keep warm.

5. Using the same large skillet, break the eggs and let them cook sunny side-up over medium to medium-low heat. Cover the pan; the eggs should be ready in about 5 minutes (don't let them overcook or they'll get rubbery).

6. If you're going to serve the avocado, now is the time to peel it, remove the pit, and sprinkle with lime (or lemon) juice, so the flesh won't darken.

7. Now assemble the huevos rancheros: on each dish place a tortilla, add an egg in the middle, and a ladle of sauce on top. If you like, garnish the dish with a quarter slice of avocado, and serve with the refried beans.

Goes well with:

- Drinks: if you feel adventurous, buy some orchata – a Mexican milk-like drink made from rice and available in some supermarkets. At a brunch or lunch serve with margaritas or coffee.
- Other recipes: serve with tortilla chips; a dash of Tabasco or other hot sauce.

Notes/Evaluation:

Orange Butter French Toast (V)

Equipment needed:
1 or 2 glass containers (or a serving dish) for step #2

Special notes:
This is a fancier version of French Toast.

Ingredients:
- 4 tablespoons butter, at room temperature
- 1 teaspoon grated orange peel (1 orange)
- 2 tablespoons orange liqueur (such as Triple Sec)
- 8 eggs
- 1/3 cup whipping cream
- 3 tablespoons maple syrup
- 3 tablespoons brandy
- 1/4 teaspoon ground nutmeg
- 1/4 teaspoon ground cinnamon
- 12 to 16 slices of French Bread
- 4 tablespoons powdered sugar
- 2 tablespoons butter, melted

Instructions:
1. In a small bowl mix 4 tablespoons of butter with the grated orange peel and orange liqueur (use a fork to mix). Set aside.
2. In a medium-size bowl beat together the next six ingredients (eggs through cinnamon). Place the slices of bread in a glass (Pyrex-type) container (you might need two) or a serving dish with sloping sides. Add the mixture over the slices – turn the slices so both sides absorb the liquid. Let stand for about 5 to 10 minutes, so the liquid is absorbed.
3. Meanwhile, in a small skillet over medium heat melt 2 tablespoons of butter.
4. Heat a frying pan or griddle to 375 degrees (or medium high heat). Brush the pan with melted butter. Cook the slices of bread until they are golden brown on both sides (about 5 to 10 minutes on each side). Sprinkle with powdered sugar.
5. Serve the French toast with the orange butter (from step #1).

Goes well with:
- Drinks: coffee or hot tea; fruit juices; even Champagne cocktail!
- Other recipes: fresh fruit or fruit cocktail; cantaloupe with prosciutto.

Notes/Evaluation:

Orange Muffins (V)

Equipment needed:

cheese grater
muffin pan
1 package paper baking cup liners
sifter
whisk (optional - you can use a fork)

Special notes:

Muffins go great anytime – at breakfast, as a dessert or a snack. They are quite easy to make and can include a variety of ingredients like various fruits (e.g., blueberries; apples) and nuts (e.g., walnuts, pecans, filberts).

Ingredients:

- 4 tablespoons melted butter
- 2 cups all purpose flour
- 1 tablespoon baking powder
- 1/2 cup sugar
- 1/2 teaspoon salt
- 1 tablespoon grated orange peel (2 oranges)
- 2 eggs
- 3/4 cup milk
- 1/4 cup orange juice (from above oranges)

Instructions:

1. Preheat the oven to 425 degrees.
2. Line a muffin pan with paper baking cup liners.
3. In a small pan melt the butter over medium to low heat.
4. Using a sifter over a bowl, sift together the flour, baking powder, sugar, and salt. Add the grated orange peel and mix well. Make a hole or well in the center of the mix.
5. In a separate bowl whisk together the two eggs, milk, orange juice, and butter.
6. Add the egg-milk mixture to the flour mixture and mix. Do NOT mix too much – the batter should be lumpy, although all the dry ingredients should be moist.
7. Fill each of the muffin cups (in place in the muffin pan) about 2/3 full of batter.
8. Bake in the oven for about 20 minutes. Test doneness by inserting a toothpick in a muffin; if ready, the toothpick should come out clean.
9. Remove the muffins from the pan as soon as you can (without personal injury). You can serve the muffins hot, or let them cool a bit.

Goes well with:

- Drinks: orange juice or other fruit juices; coffee or hot tea.
- Other recipes: great with scrambled eggs and a side order of sausage.

Notes/Evaluation:

BREAD & BREAKFAST

Pumpkin Bread (V)

Equipment needed:
3 empty 1-pound coffee cans
flour sifter

Special notes:
Even if you don't like pumpkin, you will love this bread. Like muffins, it can be eaten at almost any occasion – breakfast, brunch, a snack, or a dessert. My lovely wife makes it often (not often enough), so that the 3 empty cans are now part of our kitchen equipment.

Ingredients:
- 2-1/2 cups of sugar
- 1 teaspoon cinnamon
- 1 teaspoon salt
- 1 teaspoon grated nutmeg
- 2 teaspoons baking soda

- 4 eggs, at room temperature
- 1 cup vegetable oil
- 2/3 cup of water
- 1 cup (1 can) pumpkin puree
- 3 cups of flour
- 1/2 cup chopped walnuts (1/2 pound or less)
- vegetable shortening (Crisco)
- extra flour for dusting

Instructions:
1. Preheat the oven to 350 degrees.
2. Sift the dry ingredients into a bowl: that is, the sugar, cinnamon, salt, nutmeg, and baking soda.
3. In another bowl, beat together (with a fork) the eggs, oil, water, and pumpkin puree. Add the flour, mix well, and beat for 2 minutes. Mix in the chopped walnuts.
4. Grease well the inside of each coffee can with vegetable shortening, and lightly dust with flour. Turn can upside down to get out any excess flour.
5. Fill each coffee can half full with the batter.
6. Bake for 1 hour in the oven.
7. Let cool and remove the bread from the can. Slice and serve.

Goes well with:
- Drinks: fruit juice; coffee or hot tea.
- Other recipes: spread with cream cheese; serve with breakfast or brunch items.

Notes/Evaluation:

Scrambled Eggs (V)

Equipment needed:

spatula or wooden spoon
whisk (optional – you can use a fork)

Special notes:

I am always surprised by how many people cannot make something as simple as scrambled eggs.

Ingredients:

- 8 eggs
- 1/4 teaspoon salt
- 1/8 teaspoon freshly ground pepper
- 2 tablespoons butter
- 1 tablespoon chopped parsley (optional) or
- 2 tablespoons grated cheese (Parmesan or cheddar) (optional)

Instructions:

1. In a bowl whisk together the eggs, salt, and pepper.
2. Melt the butter in a skillet over low heat.
3. Pour the egg mixture into the skillet and with a spatula or wooden spoon stir the eggs as they cook. Cook for about 3 to 5 minutes – don't overcook or the eggs will become rubbery.
4. Serve; you can sprinkle some fresh parsley on top, or serve with a bit of grated cheese.

Goes well with:

- Drinks: coffee, hot tea, fruit juices.
- Other recipes: a side dish of sausage; sautéed mushrooms.

Notes/Evaluation:

BREAD & BREAKFAST

Western Omelet

Equipment needed:
non-stick skillet (optional)
pepper grinder (optional)

Special notes:
Omelets are another basic dish, quite simple to make, but a mystery to most men.

Ingredients:
- 2 tablespoons butter
- 1/2 cup minced green bell pepper
- 1/2 cup minced onion
- 2/3 cup finely diced ham
- 6 eggs
- 2 tablespoons milk
- 1/4 teaspoon salt
- 1/4 teaspoon freshly ground pepper

Instructions:
1. Over medium heat melt 1 tablespoon of butter in a non-stick skillet. (If you don't have a non-stick skillet, use 3 tablespoons of butter, and when melted spread the butter well across the bottom and sides.)
2. Add the bell pepper and onion and cook for 10 to 12 minutes until the vegetables are soft, stirring occasionally.
3. Add the diced ham and cook for another 5 to 7 minutes.
4. In a small bowl mix the remaining ingredients (eggs through black pepper).
5. Pour the egg mixture over the vegetables and let cook for about 10 seconds. Now comes the tricky part. Tilt the pan at a slight angle so the uncooked portion of the eggs runs to the bottom of the pan. If necessary use a spatula to move the cooked egg portion towards the center of the pan. All of this should take only a couple of minutes and sounds much more difficult than it is.
6. Take an empty plate that has been lightly buttered and place it on top of the omelet and turn the pan upside down to catch the omelet onto the plate. Now slide the upside down omelet back into the pan so its bottom will also cook. Cook for only about 30 seconds to a minute.
7. Place the omelet on a platter and divide into 4 parts; serve.

Goes well with:
- Drinks: coffee, tea, or milk.
- Other recipes: muffins; pumpkin bread.

Notes/Evaluation:

Herbs & Spices

Herbs & Spices

If you have a garden, by all means raise your own herbs, particularly basil, oregano, and rosemary. If you must buy your herbs, buy dried herbs, with the exception of parsley. "Fresh" herbs at the typical supermarket are not fresh, often not available, and overpriced.

Some of the more common herbs and spices are:

ANISE – seeds that have a licorice taste. Are used in biscottis and other cookies.

BASIL – a basic ingredient in Italian cooking. Necessary for such pasta sauces as pesto and tomato sauce. Basil is very fragrant, with a peppery flavor with overtones of mint.

BAY – in the United States this is usually California Bay, whereas in Europe it is bay laurel. In either case, the flavor is pungent with lemony overtones. Typically used as a whole (dry) leaf, that is removed at the end of cooking.

CHERVIL – has green, fern-like leaves. Gives an anise-parsley type of flavor. Is used in soups, salads, chicken dishes, and fish.

CHILI POWDER – made from ground dried chilies. Used in Mexican dishes like chili con carne.

CHIVES – dark green leaves. Is a member of the onion family. Usually used raw as a garnish. If used in a recipe, it is usually added last; is used in salads, as a topping for baked potatoes, and in omelets.

CILANTRO – see coriander.

CORIANDER – the seeds are used in a wide variety of dishes. The leaves are called cilantro and are used fresh in a wide variety of Mexican dishes, like salsa.

CUMIN – has a strong flavor – use sparingly. Used in both mid-Eastern and Mexican dishes.

DILL – has very feathery leaves. Used in fish dishes like salmon, as well as in pickling.

MARJORAM – often called "sweet" marjoram, has a very spicy yet sweet flavor. Used in seasoning meats and other dishes, and in salads.

MINT – often used as a garnish. Used in mid-Eastern cuisine. Available in a great variety of "flavors."

OREGANO – used in all sorts of Italian dishes, from salad dressings to pasta sauces.

PAPRIKA – obtained from grinding dried peppers. Can be mild or in varying degrees of hotness. Used in Hungarian dishes.

PARSLEY – used both as a garnish and to give flavor. Should be used fresh, and if possible the "Italian" type with flat leaves, rather than the more common curly leafed one.

ROSEMARY – has pine needle-like leaves. Very pungent. Quite often used in meats like roasts and roast chicken.

SAFFRON – this is probably the most expensive spice available in the supermarket. It is made from the crocus flower and gives food both a distinctive aroma and a yellowish golden color. Used in risotto, but very sparingly.

SAGE – has a smoky flavor. Used in a variety of meat and chicken dishes.

TARRAGON – also has a licorice type flavor. Use sparingly. Used in various soups and sauces, as well as roasts and shellfish recipes.

THYME – used in soups, vegetable dishes, and many meat dishes.

Wine List

Wine List

Wines are a great accompaniment to food and quite healthy in moderation, but many Americans are overwhelmed by the variety available and by the mystique that is associated with wines.

In general, you can think of wines as available in three basic types: whites, reds, and "others." White wines basically vary along a dimension of dry to sweet. Dry wines go best as a sipping wine or served with "delicate" dishes like seafood and chicken. Sweet white wines, like Muscat, go best with desserts. White wines should always be served chilled (but definitely NOT with ice cubes).

Red wines basically vary along a dimension of heartiness or robustness. Less robust wines like Beaujolais should be served cold. More robust red wines should be served at room temperature (about 55 degrees).

In the "others" category I include rose wines which can be thought of as a "mixture" of white and red, as well as special occasion wines like Sherry, Vermouth, and of course Champagne (which really needs no excuse to be drunk!).

Below are some specific suggestions, but half the fun is to discover specific wines you like. Make friends with your local wine dealer and remember that you can get some very nice wines for less than $10 a bottle.

1. White, dry:

These wines go well with dinner, particularly with seafood, or "light" main dishes, or with cheese, or simply for sipping. They should be served well-chilled. Readily available types are:

Chablis
Chardonnay
Gewurztraminer
Green Hungarian
Pinot Blanc
Pouilly-Fuisse
Rhine
Riesling
Sauvignon Blanc
Soave
Traminer
Verdicchio
White Zinfandel

2. White, sweet:

These wines are dessert wines and go well with desserts or for sipping at the end of a meal. They should be served well chilled. Readily available types are:

Muscat
Sauterne

3. Rose:

Most of these wines are on the "dry" or non-sweet side and can also be served as an accompaniment to a main dish, particularly seafood or "light" main dishes. They also go well with buffets, where a variety of foods may be served, with appetizers, and with some desserts. Serve well-chilled. For me, however, most rose's lack character and so I avoid them.

4. Red, light:

These wines, though red, are relatively mild in flavor, and sometimes tend to be on the "fruity" side. They go well with just about anything. They should be served cold but not necessarily chilled. Readily available types are:

Bardolino
Beaujolais
Cabernet
Gamay
Gamay Beaujolais

5. Red, hearty:

These are "hearty" and go well with meats and main dishes that have a strong flavor. They should be served at "room temperature," which really means on the cool side. Readily available types are:

Barbera
Barolo
Bordeaux
Cabernet Sauvignon
Chianti
Montepulciano D'Abruzzo
Petite Sirah
Pinot Noir
Shiraz

6. Other wines:

Champagne is essentially a white wine, so it should be served well chilled. It is traditionally associated with festivities like New Year's Eve, weddings, etc. but there is no reason why it cannot be enjoyed at other times of the year. Champagne can range from very dry (brut) to very sweet (demi-sec), and can be served with desserts, with cheese, but not usually as the main dinner wine.

Asti Spumante is the Italian equivalent of Champagne, but it is usually sweet and has more of a "nutty" taste. It is a wonderful wine, which I personally prefer to Champagne. Should be served well chilled.

Cold Duck is an American invention, and basically consists of a mixture of Burgundy and Champagne. Some people like it and some don't. It is often inexpensive, and you get exactly what you pay for. Should be served well chilled.

There are a number of dessert wines, like Sherry, that come in a variety of types, such as Vermouth (both dry and sweet), Marsala (also dry to sweet), and Tokay (usually quite sweet). These are usually served with dessert (including cheese) and are served at room temperature (except for the dry Vermouth famous for its part in Martinis).

Index of Cooking Terms

Index of Cooking Terms

BASTE – to brush a liquid at regular intervals (e.g., every 15 minutes) on food that is cooking. The liquid quite often contains melted butter or other fat, and the purpose of basting is to prevent the food from drying and to add flavor. A classical example is cooking a turkey in the oven.

BROIL – basically a synonym for grill, where the food is cooked with direct heat, that heat directed at one side of the food at a time (as in cooking chicken breasts).

BROWN – this term usually applies to meats or vegetables, and is a procedure that sears the food on the outside, so the natural juices and flavors stay trapped inside. Basically, it involves roasting or frying the food item at a high temperature for a short time.

CODDLE – a term typically applied to eggs when they are cooked gently in a liquid (water) that is below the boiling point, so the egg remains soft. The egg is cooked in its shell (as opposed to poached, where the egg is cooked outside its shell), and the shell is opened after the egg is cooked (see the recipe for Caesar Salad).

CORE – usually applied to tomatoes, apples, or pears, where the central core is removed, typically because it is inedible (as in a pineapple).

DICE – to cut into small, uniform cubes (about 1/8- to 1/4-inch square).

FOLD – a technique that is hard to describe but easy to do. The intent is to incorporate an ingredient into a mixture without beating or stirring. Once you have added the ingredient, you make a vertical cut with a spatula, slide the spatula across the bottom of the pan or bowl and turn it over.

JULIENNE – often applied to vegetables, it simply means to cut them into uniform matchstick shape about 1/8-inch thick and 2 inches long. (Isn't it wonderful how one word can take the place of so many!).

MINCE – to chop into very small pieces.

POACH – to cook (usually eggs out of their shell) in simmering water or other liquid.

PUREE – to press cooked food through a sieve (think baby food).

SAUTE – this comes from a French word that means "to jump." To sauté usually means to cook the food in a pan with a small amount of fat at a rather high temperature. The idea is to sear the food (for example, mushrooms or a steak) so that it does not stick.

SEAR – to brown the surface very quickly with "intense" heat.

SIMMER – to cook in liquid (like water) that has a gentle boil at the very most, but more likely the liquid is barely bubbling.

Index of Recipes

A

Albondigas soup 52
Apple pancakes 234
Avgolemono soup 56

B

Bagna Cauda (hot oil) 172
Baked pears with yogurt sauce 216
Bananas Foster 217
Barbecued chicken with lemon sauce 66
Barbequed sirloin steaks a la Bourbon 97
Barbecue tomato sauce 96
Bean dip, Tuscan 34
Beans, Tuscan style 20
Bean soup alla Bolognese 54
Beef a la Bourguignonne 98
Beets, marinated 183
Biscotti, chocolate 220
Brandy Alexander 200
Bread and tomato salad 41
Bread pudding (capirotada) 218
Broccoli, Italian 181
Bronx cocktail 201
Bruschetta 14

C

Caesar salad 36
Cantaloupe and prosciutto 15
Caper and olive dip (Tapenade) 33
Capirotada (bread pudding) 218
Caponata 16
Caprese salad 40
Caramel custard (Crème Brulee) 222
Caribbean style chicken 67
Carrots, simple 191
Carrots, stir fried 192
Carrots with cheese 173
Celery, cheese stuffed 17
Champagne cocktail 202

Champagne punch 203
Cheese, flaming Kasseri 21
Cheesecake with peaches, Valerie's 228
Cherries jubilee 219
Chicken and vegetables, stir-fried 90
Chicken cashew, stir fry 91
Chicken, garlic 86
Chicken, hunter style 84
Chicken in white wine 68
Chicken, Jerusalem style 81
Chicken Marsala 70
Chicken, Mediterranean 82
Chicken, Moroccan style 71
Chicken piccata 72
Chicken roasted with vegetables 88
Chicken rolls 73
Chicken with artichoke hearts 74
Chicken with mushrooms 75
Chicken with mushrooms Two 76
Chicken with pea-pods 77
Chicken with rice 87
Chiles rellenos 174
Chiles rellenos with Pico de Gallo sauce 176
Chili con carne 100
Chinese chicken 80
Chinese chicken with mushrooms 78
Chinese fried rice 158
Chinese rice 159
Chocolate biscotti 220
Chocolate, hot Mexican 209
Chocolate ice cream, white 229
Cioppino 114
Clams Casino 18
Clams oreganate 19
Cobbler, peach 224
Cocoa, coffee, and crème 204
Corn soup, Veronica's Mexican 61
Cream cheese dessert 223
Crème Brulee 222

D

Daiquiris, peach frozen 207
Dutch baby 235

E

Eggplant medley with mint dressing 178
Eggplant salad, Greek 38
Eggs Benedict 236
Eggs, ranch style (huevos rancheros) 240
Eggs, scrambled 245

F

Fagioli alla Toscana 20
Fajitas, pork 104
Fettucine Alfredo 128
Fettucine with lemon sauce 129
Fillet of sole with garlic sauce 116
Fish fillets in tomato sauce 117
Flaming Kasseri cheese 21
Focaccia 238
Formaggio crema 223
French garlic salad dressing 37
French onion soup 55
French toast 239
French toast with orange butter 242
Fried rice, Chinese 158
Frittata, zucchini 196
Frozen blue margarita 205
Frozen Imperial cocktail 206
Frozen peach daiquiris 207

G

Garbanzo beans, marinated 26
Garlic chicken 86
Garlic, French salad dressing 37
Garlic mushrooms 180
Garlic toast 22
Gin Fizz, Ramos 211
Greek Avgolemono soup 56
Greek eggplant salad 38

Greek salad 39
Grilled salmon steaks 118
Guacamole 23

H

Huevos rancheros 240
Hummus and pita bread 24

I

Ice cream pie, white and green 230
Ice cream, vanilla with rum sauce 227
Ice cream, white chocolate 229
Insalata Caprese 40
Irish coffee 208
Italian broccoli 181
Italian vegetables 182

J

Jerusalem style chicken 81

L

Leek and potato soup 62
Linguine alla Giorgio 132
Linguine al pesto 130
Linguine, Torino style 134
Linguine with garlic and hazelnut sauce 136
Linguine with white clam sauce 135
Linguine with zucchini and green onions 138
London broil 101

M

Margarita, blue frozen 205
Marinated beets 183
Marinated garbanzo beans 26
Marinated grilled shrimp 119
Marinated zucchinis 27
Marinated zucchinis and olives 28

Mediterranean chicken 82
Mexican corn soup, Veronica's 61
Mexican hot chocolate 209
Mexican meatball soup 52
Moo Goo Gai Pan 78
Moroccan vegetables 184
Mozzarella in carrozza 29
Mushrooms, garlic 180
Muffins, orange 243
Mussels and clams, steamed with chorizo 126

N

Nicoise, salad 44
Nonna's rice soup 57

O

Omelet, Western 246
Orange butter French toast 242
Orange muffins 243

P

Pancakes, apple 234
Panzanella salad 41
Peach cobbler 224
Peaches, stuffed 226
Peach smoothee 210
Peanut butter chicken 83
Pears with yogurt sauce, baked 216
Penne with tomato sauce 139
Pepper and onion salad 42
Pepper steak 102
Peppers with olives and anchovies 30
Polenta 160
Polenta with ham 161
Pollo alla cacciatore 84
Pollo all'aglio 86
Pollo con riso 87
Pork chops in white wine 103

Pork fajitas 104
Pork medallions with mustard-cream sauce 106
Pork roast, Piemonte style 108
Potatoes Anna 185
Potatoes, roasted 188
Potatoes, roasted garlic 187
Pudding, bread (Capirotada) 218
Pudding, rice 225
Pumpkin bread 244
Punch, Champagne 203
Punch, red wine (Sangria) 213

Q

Quesadillas 31
Quick vegetable medley 186

R

Ramos Gin Fizz 211
Rib eye roast 109
Rice and beef teriyaki 162
Rice, Chinese 159
Rice pudding 225
Rice soup, Nonna's 59
Rice with mid-Eastern sauce 164
Rice with sautéed mixed vegetables 165
Risotto 166
Risotto with mushrooms 167
Risotto with pesto 170
Risotto with red wine 168
Roasted chicken with vegetables 88
Roasted garlic potatoes 187
Roasted potatoes 188

S

Salad Nicoise 44
Salad with honey mustard vinaigrette 46
Salmon steaks, grilled 118
Salty dog 212

Sangria 213
Sauteed yellow squash 189
Sauteed zucchinis 190
Scallops with lemon and wine 120
Scrambled eggs 245
Shrimp, marinated grilled 119
Shrimp tempura 122
Shrimp with aioli 121
Simple carrots 191
Sole with garlic sauce 116
Spaghetti alla Bolognese 140
Spaghetti alla carbonara 141
Spaghetti alla Puttanesca 142
Spaghetti alla Toscana 143
Spaghetti al tonno 144
Spaghetti sauce a la Marinara 145
Spaghetti sauce a la Portofino 146
Spaghetti sauce with mushrooms 147
Spaghetti with aglio e olio 148
Spaghetti with anchovies, capers and olives 149
Spaghetti with gorgonzola and walnuts 152
Spaghetti with mushrooms and sausage 150
Spaghetti with salsa fresca 153
Spaghetti with sausage 154
Split pea soup 58
Squash, yellow sautéed 189
Steak au poivre 102
Steak with cognac sauce 110
Steamed mussels and clams with chorizo 126
Stir fried carrots 192
Stir fried chicken and vegetables 90
Stir fried chicken cashew 91
Stir fried vegetables 193
Stracciatella alla Romana 60
Stuffed chicken breasts 92
Stuffed peaches 226

T

Tabbouleh 32
Tapenade 33
Tempura, shrimp 122
Tomato and basil salad 47
Tomato salad 48
Trout baked in parchment paper 124
Tuscan bean dip 34

V

Valerie's cheesecake with peaches 228
Vanilla ice cream with rum sauce 227
Veal scaloppine with Marsala 111
Vegetable medley 194
Vegetable medley, quick 186
Vegetables, Italian 182
Vegetables, Moroccan 184
Vegetable soup, winter 64
Vegetables, stir fried 193
Veronica's Mexican corn soup 61
Vichyssoise 62
Vinaigrette, honey mustard 46

W

Waldorf salad 49
Western omelet 246
White and green ice cream pie 230
White chocolate ice cream 229
Winter vegetable soup 64

Z

Zabaglione al Rum 232
Ziti with broccoli 155
Zucchini frittata 196
Zucchinis and olives, marinated 28
Zucchinis, marinated 27
Zucchinis, sautéed 190
Zucchinis stuffed with sausage and provolone 195